WORLD WAR II COMBAT VETERANS

Stories of Commitment and Valor

TABLE OF CONTENTS

Dedication

This book is dedicated to my friend, Jack Stephan, Navy veteran who has served his country (1953-1955) and community with pride and distinction. He served on-board two aircraft carriers, the USS Sicily and USS Point Cruz. After shore duty he served in the reserves and retired as a Lieutenant. Jack returned home to Columbus, Ohio to nurture his family and business and was called upon by many community leaders to *give advice, leadership and guidance to various community endeavors.*

Jack served as president:

- The University Club Board of Trustees
- The Columbus Academy Board of Trustees, Distinguished Alumnus Award, 1984
- The Golf Club Board of Governors
- Rocky Fork Hunt and Country Club Board of Trustees
- Gladden Community House Board of Trustees
- Glenn Rest Memorial Estates Board of Trustees
- The Lakes Golf and Country Club Board of Trustees
- Independent Insurance Agents of Columbus Board of Trustees

JACK STEPHAN-THANK YOU FOR YOUR SERVICE

Acknowledgements

A special thank you to the genius of Jim lifter, who created the cover, formatted and edited the stories of these heroic World War II combat veterans.

I am also grateful to Libby Patrick, Warren Motts, Bette Young, and Jack Stephan who provided me with the referrals to these courageous warriors.

To my wife Rita, who is always present to give me encouragement and sound advice.

To my old buddy, Jim McCarty, USMC who is the personification of a raconteur- "a person who is skilled in relating stories and anecdotes interestingly". A true friend and mentor!

Author Contact Information:

To purchase additional copies of this book search for "WW II Combat Veterans" at www.amazon.com

E-mail: dcohen1935@gmail.com

Phone: (614) 861-0778

Prologue

Why Honor These Veterans

If it weren't for the 10 million Americans who served in our armed forces during World War II we wouldn't be living in the world as we know it today. The word freedom might just be a dream, not reality.

In Tom Brokaw's brilliant book, "The Greatest Generation", he profiles those who grew up in the US during the deprivation of the Great Depression and then went on to fight in World War II, as well as those whose productivity within the war's home front made a decisive contribution to the war.

Brokaw goes on to say "it is, I believe, the greatest generation (born 1901-1927) any society has ever produced". He argued that these men and women fought not for fame and recognition, but because it was the "right thing to do". Donald Dunn, Dan Carmichael, Don Jakeway, Fred Zacharias, Milt Mapou, Eddie Leibbrand, Leila Morrison and Mike Pohorilla each told me—**"The commitment to serve our country in time of war is something they have never regretted, and the honor was theirs."**

They certainly are the poster children for THE GREATEST GENERATION

Picture in a Frame

Away in an attic
'neath a blanket of dust,
Rests a hump- topped treasure chest
whose hinges now rust.

Though mostly forgotten
the coffer stands with great pride.
Aware of the heirlooms
it harbors safely inside.

Jim McCarty

December 8th, 1941, the then President of the United States of America, Franklin Delano Roosevelt, acting in conjunction with the U.S. Congress, declared war against the Imperial Empire of Japan. This crucial and unwavering declaration thrust America into the tenacious role of "active combatant" in what would become known as, the "deadliest military conflict in recorded history"; World War II.

At the time of America's incursion into the brutal, hands-on warfare, the United States population stood at a respectable 131 million people. When the Godawful carnage drew to a close on August 14, 1945, (V-J Day) – Victory in Japan, 419,000 U.S.

military combatants, three percent of the nation's citizenry, had perished. While this fact is completely true, it is far from being truly complete. What is missing from the observation, is that during the scant half decade of death and destruction, three percent of the U.S. population had indeed perished. What is not conveyed, however, is that due to the carnage abroad, the constant focus on overseas happenings by the United States news outlets, and commodity rationing on the home front, 100 percent of American society at the time, had changed both their psyche and their personal lives forever. And so, what people say, must be true. That is, history does in fact repeat itself.

For, when "the War to End All Wars"; World War I, drew to a close, November 11, 1918, and the troops returned home following their overseas deployments, they were not the same boys and girls who left the States only a year or two earlier. Because of their newfound experiences in the military, their hopes and dreams, psyches and personalities had changed…forever! Those carefree boys and girls quickly evolved into serious men and women. So much so was this transformation, that even the most popular hit tune back in the day, ballyhooed the metamorphous; *"How Ya Gonna Keep 'Em Down on the Farm After They've Seen Paree?"* – Andrew Bird. Changing environments and altering circumstances do in fact change the person! So, you may ask, how does one uncover or discover the new personality of the war-fighter who returns home from the front?

Proudly displayed on living room walls, fireplace mantles, bedroom dressers, corner bookshelves, glass front bureaus, or carefully stored in an old hump-top steamer trunk tucked away in someone's attic, are keepsake photos. Heirlooms of cherished family members who stepped forward to serve our country during the First and Second World Wars, and who thereby earned the nation's gratitude, strong praise, and recognition that "all gave some, and some gave all". These photos are clues to a soldier's new identity. For behind every photo, there lies a story. And within each story, there lies a truth.

In spite of the fact that endless feet of film have been shot and developed, a myriad of documentaries have been produced, numerous books have been written, and countless versions of World War II have been related, there still remains a few faces in those personal family frames of distinction whose stories have yet to be told.

Acting on his cunning resourcefulness and artful skills of detection, author, I. David Cohen, has pried open several old hump-topped steamer trunks, reached deep inside a few tarnished and weathered picture frames, and discovered photographs of eight such WWII military veterans living in his own backyard of Columbus, Ohio. Special people from a special time, who rose to the occasion, and did special things to keep America safe and free.

Mr. Cohen admirably introduces us to these unique war-fighters from World War II as he masterfully relates their tales in this exciting, thought-provoking manuscript, "Stories of Commitment and Valor".

Read it now, and share it with friends. You will be happy you did!

Cpl. James P. McCarty, USMC

Jim McCarty - THANK YOU FOR YOUR SERVICE

Donald Dunn

In 1915 Janet Campbell and Harold Dunn were married. Over the next 15 years they produced five beautiful and talented children. Gordon was the oldest, followed by Harold and Bob. Donald, known as Donnie, became the youngest son followed by little sister Mary Janet. Today, Donald and Mary Janet are the survivors of the original five. Donald's mother was a hard-working loving wife who devoted her life to raising her children. His father, a graduate of Wesleyan University in Middletown, Connecticut, was employed by the West Penn Power Company in Pittsburgh, Pennsylvania. They resided in Ben Avon Heights which is a small town 7 miles north of Pittsburgh. Donald refers to his family as not being wealthy but as upper middle America. They were hard-core Republicans.

When Donald was born in 1923 the country was in the midst of a tremendous economic boom - - the roaring 20s.However, it all came to an end in September, 1929 when the stock market crashed and billions of dollars were lost. Bad times followed. The Great Depression of the 1930s was upon us and lasted until the United States entered World War II in December, 1941.

Donald's family was hard-hit by the depression but his father continued to work for the West Penn Power Company and they were able to survive.

During Donald's school years he was neither a good athlete nor a good student. His father constantly admonished him for staying in his room playing his trumpet when he felt he should be studying his lessons. His father encouraged him to study more but he still remained a C student. To this day Donald admits that he was a disappointment to his father because of his lack of achievement. However, he does note that his father would be shocked, but pleasantly surprised today, to learn of his war record, and also know that he founded and directed a highly successful plastics company!

A good friend of Donald's father was an attorney and politician, Louis Johnson. In 1935, when Donald was 12 years old, he along with his father had the opportunity to meet Mr. Johnson at a gathering in downtown Pittsburgh. Mr. Johnson advocated universal military education and training, rearmament, and expansion of military aviation. In those days he was one of a small number of people who felt the United States was headed into another war. The government took his advice and from 1937 to 1940 he became Assistant Secretary of War. Later, in 1948, he became the second United States Secretary of Defense. As far as Donald was concerned the highlight of their gathering was that Mr. Johnson gave him a German Shepherd dog who he named Fritz. Meeting Louis Johnson was a real treat for Donald. One that he will never forget.

In June, 1941 Donald graduated from high school and entered Wesleyan University. After completing one year as a freshman, he began his sophomore year in the fall of 1942. The likelihood at the time, was that most male students would be drafted and serve in the armed forces. There were few exceptions. There were no college deferments. One day Donald read an article in the University's newspaper discussing ski troops in the Army. The article stated that the Army was going to form a Mountain Division and were looking for people who knew how to ski. All applicants were to write a letter to the National Ski Patrol, and describe their personal skiing expertise.

Donald believes he and all of the other candidates probably exaggerated their prowess as good skiers. He could ski but he certainly wasn't an expert. The Army accepted all applicants as they were desperate to begin the 10th Mountain Division, and needed manpower in a hurry. At the time Donald thought it would be fun to be part of the 10th Mountain Division. It ended up, however, not being any fun at all. In the spring of 1943, he reported for induction into the Army. An experience that changed his life forever.

 A year or so earlier his second oldest brother Harold, became a Navigator in a bomber squadron, and rose to the rank of Major. His brother Bob, became a Captain and an aircraft pilot, and was serving in the Pacific when the Japanese attacked Pearl Harbor. Three sons serving in the military from one family – much for the family to worry about.

10th Mountain Division Training

The 10th Mountain Division (Alpine) was formed on July 10, 1943. to receive intense specialized training for fighting in the mountains and arctic conditions. Their purpose was to prepare war fighters to engage the enemy in Arctic Mountain conditions and terrain. The US Army authorized the formation of the platoon-sized ski patrols in November, 1940. The initial thought was to have ten Mountain Divisions, but personnel shortages revised the goal to three.

The 10th Mountain Division was the only one brought into active duty.

The Division had equipment specifically selected and designed for deep snow operations and sub- zero winter weather, that specialized in snow operations with winter weather gear such as white camouflage and skis specially designed for the Division.

Their training at Camp Hale, near Pando, Colorado included snowshoeing, skiing and rock climbing. They also learned cold – weather survival tactics, such as building snow caves to capture some degree of warmth, and to block the wind.

During training the 10th Mountain Division lived in the mountains for weeks, and worked in altitudes of up to 13,000 feet. Five to six feet of snow, and temperatures that dropped to 20° below zero at night, were common place. Donald humorously recalls, that the "F" expletive was used quite often to express their feelings.

From the day they arrived at Camp Hale they all wondered where and when they would be shipped overseas to fight the Germans. In a year they would know.

Shortly after arriving at Camp Hale, Donald was informed that his brother Bob had disappeared while on a flight near Pearl Harbor. He requested permission from his commanding officer, Capt. Bill Bowerman, if he could take leave to visit his mother back in Pennsylvania. Captain Bowerman suggested that they wait and see if they could recover his brother's body, and if that happened, he would then grant Donald's request to return home. Months passed and his brother's body was not recovered and Donald never did return home to comfort his grieving mother. After the war, Donald had no additional contact with Captain Bowerman.

Years later, Donald learned that Bowerman had become the track coach for the University of Oregon. One morning while coach Bowerman was eating a waffle for breakfast. he observed the shape of the waffle and it dawned upon him that the configuration of the waffle would make a good sole for a track shoe. Bowerman showed the design to his leading track star, Phil Knight, which resulted in the two of them founding a small foot-ware company which they called, Nike. Incidentally, today, Nike grosses in excess of $35 billion a year in revenues.

Heading to War in Italy

In the summer of 1944, the 10th Mountain Division packed up and headed for Texas. They remained in Texas for four months awaiting further orders. In mid- December they shipped out and headed towards Europe – not being told their final destination. On December 24, they landed in Naples, Italy. The next day they boarded a ship and headed north to Livorno which was located at the foot of the mountains which the Germans held. Livorno, Italy is 273 miles north of Naples and 50 miles west of Florence. They were told that their mission was to help retake the Apennine Mountain Chain which stretched some 25 miles from west to east. The immediate objective was to capture Mount Belvedere which had the most rugged terrain. Donald's unit was not involved in the assault of Mount Belvedere which was both brutal and bloody with many lost lives. Luckily for him and the members of his platoon they were held in reserve.

Several weeks later, one- night, Donald's platoon was ordered to climb a small mountain and attempt to capture a

Sentry. It was cold and snowy. The weather was so miserable they couldn't see their hands in front of their face, let alone spot a Sentry and try to capture him. It was a futile effort and according to Donald it was one of the dumbest ideas the Army ever had sending them out to try to capture a Sentry in such weather conditions.

Following that ordeal, his unit was ordered to clear the German held village of Cutigliano. The date was March 3rd and this was Donald's first foray into battle. A year and a half of training now would be put to the test. With rifles, fixed bayonets and grenades their mission was made clear – **Rid the town of the Germans!!!**

The Germans knew they were present and fired everything they could possibly bombard them with including firing 88 mm artillery shells which came reigning down on them, screaming and screeching, causing great confusion and fear. It was not only intimidating, but also lethal. The German snipers were also trying to pick them off one by one – – – his platoon had to hide behind trees to avoid being killed. A fellow soldier, Gregory Vaccarino, a tough Italian became so scared while in battle he panicked and ran into an open space and was immediately shot and killed. Our troops were trained to keep their emotions in check but apparently fright and flight took over which cost him his life. Donald was astounded that this big tough Italian may not be as tough as he appeared to be.

After claiming the town of Cutigliano his platoon proceeded to the village of Castle Diano and cleared the German soldiers. At this point, Donald was able to settle his nerves, fears and anxieties, so that he could do his job more effectively. In just two skirmishes he had become a combat veteran.

In April, 1945 the US Army was aligned along the boot of Italy in a push to defeat the Germans and move north into Germany. Our troops were preparing for one final thrust. Mount Belvedere had been taken on February 19th of 1945 and the next objective for the 10th Mountain Division was the capturing of Hill 775 (775 feet tall) just north of Mount Belvedere.

On April 15, 1945 his platoon was assigned their most important mission-- retake Hill 775.Normally, a lieutenant would be their platoon leader but through a series of events, their first platoon leader had a nervous breakdown and his replacement had no battle experience. The members of Donald's platoon became quite concerned that they were going into battle without an experienced leader. Donald's fellow soldiers insisted that he speak with their company commander, Captain William Faust, and express their concerns about who was going to lead them into battle. After listening to Donald's comments, he made the decision "Sergeant Dunn, you are the new platoon leader". Donald certainly did not want that position for the fact that he had never had any experience in being a leader. He also knew that the platoon leader was usually the one that was killed first and being killed was of little interest to him. However, an order is an order and off they went into battle. Staff Sergeant Dunn, with his platoon of 40 men, started fighting their way towards Hill 775. Along the way they lost 20 men.

The orders of this mission were precise to the minute. They had to be in position at the bottom of Hill 775 at exactly 3:50 PM when the allies would begin bombing the hill. Their orders were plain and simple – at 4 PM make an assault and capture the hill. They had been fighting all day and were exhausted as well as losing a number of soldiers – but the mission had to be accomplished and they were dedicated to taking back Hill 775. That afternoon his men were ready for the challenge.

They started marching single file climbing the mountain and clearing the Germans. They ascended about one fourth of the hill when they experienced the ravages of the machine gun the Germans had positioned on top of the hill. Bullets were flying everywhere. They were in open mountain terrain, nowhere to hide and their only option was to lay prone on the ground until the gunfire ceased. They were crawling on their stomachs up the hill and to their horror behind them was a German sniper shooting at each of them. The  sniper shot every soldier; some were simply wounded, others were killed. Donald was wounded with a bullet through his right shoulder and chest. There was not an exit wound, which made him believe he was going to bleed internally and simply die on the spot. However, he was able to continue to fight and at the same time with other platoons joining them they accomplished taking Hill 775. These combined platoons enabled the 10th Mountain Division along with other Army units to continue north to take subsequent hills in their quest to break the German lines.

Once Hill 775 had been retaken Donald's platoon descended the mountain and walked across the open field back to their base camp. Even though in terrible pain Donald was able to make it back safely. Along the way, they witnessed unspeakable carnage and the ravages of war. The smells of death were similar to that of a Chicago beef slaughtering house.

Upon returning to camp Donald was proud to tell Captain Faust they had accomplished their mission and that he was proud of his men. The Captain then asked Donald what he was going to do next and Donald's response was quite simple "I'm probably going to die so perhaps I should find an ambulance and see if they can save my life".

Donald did find an ambulance that took him to a field hospital where they operated and removed the bullet wound. He stayed in the field hospital for a few weeks. By that time the 10th Mountain Division had boarded their troop ship and headed back to the United States.

Of course, his outfit had left without him. As a result of him being left behind he was granted a furlough and was instructed to wait until they could assign him to a ship to return to the United States. The usual confusion of the Army didn't make it happen quickly so he was temporarily assigned as a supply Sergeant in Naples. Donald remained in Naples for a couple of months – December, 1945. As a nice gesture, the Army gave him a free train trip to Switzerland where he had never visited before. He fell in love with the country. By this time his health was improved and fully recovered from being shot. His thinking at the time was that there was not any big rush to get back to the United States.

During his stint in Naples he was introduced to the Opera and loved going to various performances. One night at the Opera House Donald was privileged to hear Gracie Fields perform. She was an English actress, singer, comedienne and star of both cinema and music hall. She spent her later part of her life on the Isle of Capri, Italy. On this particular evening the Opera House was filled with soldiers from all nations and at the end of her performance she asked soldiers from each country represented to sing their National Anthems. Donald was so proud to be one of the American soldiers who stood up and sang the Star-Spangled Banner. In the middle of December,1945 Staff Sergeant Donald G. Dunn boarded a troopship and headed for the United States. He had arrived in Naples, Italy on Christmas Eve,1944 and arrived back in New York Harbor on Christmas eve, 1945. It was an emotional experience for him arriving into New York Harbor and passing by the Stature of Liberty. The tugboats and other small boats sounded their horns welcoming them back to the United States.

The 10th Mountain Division, in World War II, arrived in Italy from Texas with 8,500 troops and fought in the roughest terrains of Italy. In total, the 10th Mountain Division had 13,000 fighting men in Italy. They saw combat in Cutigliano, Battle of Monte Castello, Monte Della Torraccia-Mount Belvedere, Canolle, Mongiorgio, Torbole and Nago. 992 were killed in action, 4,154 wounded in 114 days of combat.

For Donald G. Dunn's commitment and service to our country he was awarded:

The Silver Star Medal----Awarded for singular acts of valor or heroism over a brief period, such as one or two days.
The Bronze Star Medal----A decoration awarded to members of the United States Armed Forces for either heroic achievement, heroic service, meritorious achievement or meritorious service in a combat zone.
The Purple Heart----Awarded both for wounds received in action against the enemy and for meritorious performance of duty. Donald received two Purple Hearts.

I asked Donald how being a member of the 10th Mountain Division fighting in the rugged terrain of Italy affected him. He said that the war helped him have more confidence in himself – the confidence led him to become a better student, to believe in himself better and he also feels that we all need to make sacrifices when necessary to keep our nation free. DONALD G. DUNN----------A TRUE WAR HERO

LIFE AFTER WORLD WAR II

After being discharged from the Army Donald returned home to Pennsylvania to reunite with his mother and sister. Soon after, he traveled to Tennessee to visit the parents of fellow platoon leader, Harden Shelby, who had been mortally wounded in the capturing of Hill 775 in Italy. It was both a sad but rewarding visit he had with their family. The memories of death and heroism were still fresh in Donald's mind. He was able to express his grief as well as his admiration for a fellow soldier who also fought valiantly and was also a true war hero!

In January, 1946 Donald returned to Wesleyan University to continue his education. He wanted to live in his old fraternity house but the only available sleeping accommodations available were to share a room with a Columbus, Ohio native Charles Loving. On the very first day he met Charles, Donald recalled visiting Columbus, Ohio back in 1939 when his brother Bob was attending Ohio State. Donald also remembered meeting his brother Bob's roommate, Don Scott. As fate would have it, both Bob and Don Scott became members of the US Army Air Corps. **Both were killed in action**. On November 1, 1943 The Ohio State University trustees named their new airport Don Scott Field in honor of the former all – American football player who died in a bomber crash in England on October 1, 1943.

Donald and Charles Loving continued their education and before they graduated Charles introduced Donald to his future wife, Mary Elizabeth Altmaier, a native of Columbus, Ohio. Mary and Donald were married in 1948, moved to Chicago to begin Donald's career as a management trainee with Connecticut General life Insurance Company. The couple remained in Chicago for one year before Charles Loving suggested that Donald and his wife return to Columbus so he and Charles could form a partnership to enter the low housing construction business. However, after returning to Columbus, Charles informed Donald that he was no longer interested in forming the business partnership. OPPS!!!! Donald was now unemployed.

Knowing that he wanted to start his own business, Donald visited the Columbus Chamber of Commerce and inquired about businesses or companies that he might join. They directed him to an old dump of a building in German Village where he met a character by the unusual name of Borden Hively. The name of his company was called PLASKOLITE. They manufactured plastic drinking straws which were produced from an old rickety machine the size of a small table. Within a few days Donald invested $9,000 and became a shareholder of this fledgling company. As a 27-year-old with no business experience, his first duties were to clean the bathroom and pack straws for delivery. The business struggled for the next three or four months when Hively announced that they were out of money. Apparently, Mr. Hively had used Donald's $9,000 to pay his personal bills – they were broke. In frustration Donald fired Borden leaving him alone to run and manage the company without any funds. Donald's thinking at the time "now what will I do?" As a matter of desperation Donald visited a local banker and requested a $15,000 loan. When the banker reviewed his financial statements, which were dripping with red ink, he promptly denied the loan request without a co- signature from Donald's wife. Mary Elizabeth readily agreed and the business was saved.

 In the early 1950s Donald teamed up with a friend, Norris Olson and together they ran the company making drinking straws. They both had creative minds and could envision different uses of plastics. They eventually made the mold- lenses for florescent lighting fixtures which launched their company to the next level. As Donald noted "we were a great team".

In 1962, they purchased property on Joyce Avenue and hired famous Columbus architect, Dan Carmichael, to design a 45,000 ft.² building. Donald and Norris co – managed the company, worked hand – in- hand for two more years. In 1964, Norris decided to resign and move to Vero Beach Florida. Donald purchased his stock and now was the top executive at the company.

In 1967, as another enterprise, Donald built the Columbus Indoor Tennis Club which became the premier indoor tennis facility in Central, Ohio. In 1969, as president of the Buckeye Boys Ranch Board of Trustees, Donald turned a long – time dream into the solution to a fund- raising problem. The board was looking for a money – making project and Donald had been thinking about donating a tennis court to the Ranch for the boys' use. Having had a deep interest in tennis the idea of a professional tennis tournament at the Ranch evolved. In the summer of 1970, the first Buckeye Tennis Championship was held with an eight man draw with a $12,500 purse. It was played on a Dynaturf court donated by Donald, the first of two he gave the Ranch. Donald has believed and participated in the idea of private fund raising through his work with the Ranch and his efforts on its behalf throughout the community.

In reference to his company in 2012, Donald remarked "within his team is a remarkable spirit of cooperation, loyalty, decency, hard work, boldness and unselfishness. This attitude has permeated throughout the rest of the work force and is the true reason why PLASKOLITE is poised to remain the industry leader in the years ahead".
When people ask who started PLASKOLITE Donald always says "my wife and I".

THE REST OF THE STORY

From 1949 through 1957 Donald and Mary Elizabeth welcomed the birth of five children: Bob, Andy, Jim, Gardner and Nancy. Today, Donald is blessed to have 13 grandchildren and 22 great grandchildren.

Looking back upon Donald's life he is an individual who came from a middle-class family, with solid moral values, who gained confidence as a soldier while leading others into battle. As a decorated war- hero he has taken the skills he learned in the Army and applied them to the challenges he faced in building a tremendously successful plastics company. He is a man of vision and dedication. His contribution to the business community and philanthropy cannot be measured only in dollars and cents. He truly is a man for all seasons who has made a difference in the lives of all the people he touched.

Donald G. Dunn – Thank You For Your Service

Don Jakeway

Don Jakeway, known as Jake by his friends, was born and raised on a small farm in Johnstown, Ohio. Since his youth his father had been a farmer, and the family made their modest living growing garden crops and keeping a few livestock. Jake, one of six children, worked all the time through school and was an outstanding athlete. He was known for his fiery temper, always wanting to be the best at everything he did. Don, at age 18, enlisted in the Airborne in October, 1942. Small at 138 pounds in High School, he quickly built himself up to 180 pounds during the first few months of his paratrooper training.

AIRBORNE HISTORY

The concept of Airborne Troops, though attributed to the military planners of World War II, was not quite that new. There were such ideas in the minds of one or two of the Allied General Staff during the final days of World War I.

However, the scope of such an operation would have been quite limited.

In the early days of World War II, and well before the United States entered the conflict, the British were already organizing and training Airborne units such as paratroopers, glider troops, and various airborne support units, which later became "The British 1st Airborne Division". The planner and trainer was Sir Frederick Browning.

General Browning visited the United States at the invitation of a few farsighted individuals on the General Staff, and succeeded in presenting his ideas. Shortly thereafter a "Parachute Test Platoon" was organized, and through their pioneering, the feasibility of Airborne Troops was proven. The rapidity with which the 1st Division of American Airborne Troops was formed was amazing. The first units received their baptism of fire in North Africa, Sicily and Italy, proving themselves beyond any shadow of a doubt, to be far superior to conventional combat troops.

With the advent of the planning of "Operation Overlord", (D- DAY), General Browning again entered the picture and with his staff, met with the American General Staff creating the first Allied Airborne Army. It came into being. It consisted of the British 1st Airborne Division, the American 82nd and the 101st Airborne Divisions. The free French and Polish were also represented a short while later, and small units of each were attached to the 1st Allied Airborne Army.

PARATROOPER TRAINING

After spending the night in the old Fort Hayes Hotel in Columbus, Ohio Don and one of his close high school friends Paul boarded a train and headed south. At various stops at camps along the way, a group of nine other enlisted men joined them. Soon afterwards they were given physicals and only Paul and Don passed. They arrived in camp Toccoa, Georgia in early October, 1942. They received their shots and endured yet another physical examination.

They also got a hint of what was to come, a jump from a 60-foot high mock tower. Shortly thereafter, to receive basic infantry training, they were transferred to Camp Blanding, Florida for the next 13 weeks. From Camp Blanding the next stop was Fort Benning, Georgia in preparation to becoming a paratrooper. Each of them needed to complete "five qualifying jumps". Don and Paul passed with flying colors. Over the next few weeks Don attended demolition school, compass reading school and airplane identification school. With these accomplishments he was well on his way to become a paratrooper. They both served in Normandy and they are still friends today.

In June 1943, Don was transferred to Camp Mackall, North Carolina where he trained in preparation for jumping into combat. The training was both rigorous, and mind numbing. Don learned how to handle his rifle, grenades and the use of mortar in combat as well as how to identify various foreign objects. He went on field trials existing on K rations and limited drinking water. He had to learn and understand how to identify various landmarks that would be helpful to him while in battle. Physically he was required to shimmy up a forty- foot rope only using his hands.

Once he reached the top, he had to grasp the rope by his legs with his arms spread outwards. He needed to hold that position for a few moments. Each recruit had to repeat this rope climbing challenge four or five times a day. The rigorous training was necessary to weed out those who either didn't want to or couldn't perform the tasks necessary to become a paratrooper. The dropout rate was one third. During his stay at Camp Mackall his regiment of 6,000 men thought they were going to the Pacific and eventually Japan. To prepare for this eventuality they trained in the swamps of North Carolina. Their training was brutal in that they had to navigate through muddy swamps encountering alligators as well as poisonous snakes. They were told "you are preparing for what is to come".

Donald Jakeway
Company "H" 508th Infantry Regiment

The Parachutists Creed

I volunteered as a parachutist, fully realizing the hazards of my chosen service, and by my thoughts and actions will always uphold the prestige, honor, and rich esprit-de –corps of the only volunteer branch of the Army.

I realize that a parachutist is not merely a soldier who arrives by a parachute to fight, but an elite shock trooper, and that his country expects him to march further and faster, to fight harder, to be more self-reliant, and to soldier better than any other soldier.

---

*Parachutists of all Allied Armies belong to
this great brotherhood.*

*I shall never fail my fellow comrades by
  shirking any duty of training, but will always
  keep myself mentally and physically fit and
  shoulder my full share of the task, whatever
  it may be.*

*I shall always accord my superiors my fullest
  loyalty and I will always bear in mind the
  sacred trust I have in the lives of men, I will
  lead into battle.*

*I shall show other soldiers, by my military
  courtesy to my superior officer and non—
  commissioned officers, by my neatness in
  dress, by my care for my weapons and
  equipment, that I am a picked and well-
  trained soldier.*

*I shall endeavor by my soldierly appearance,
  military bearing and behavior, to reflect the
  high standards of training and morale of
  parachute troops*

*I shall respect the abilities of my enemies, I
  will fight fairly and with all my might.
  Surrender is not in my creed.*

*I shall display a higher degree of initiative
  that is required of the other troops, and will*

*fight on to my objective and mission, though
I may be the lone survivor.*

*I will prove my ability as a fighting man,
against the enemy of the field of battle, not
by quarreling with my commanders in arm,
or by bragging about my deeds, thus
needlessly arousing jealousy, and resentment
against parachute troops.*

*I shall always realize, that battles are won by
an army fighting as a team, that I fight, and
blaze a path into battle, or others to follow,
and carry the battle on.*

*I belong to the finest unit in the Army. By my
appearance, actions, and battlefield deeds
alone, I speak for my fighting ability. I will
strive to uphold the honor and prestige of my
outfit, making my country proud of me, and
the unit to which I belong.*

*US paratroopers, provide the enemy, with a
maximum opportunity, to give their lives for
their country.*

In December, 1943 Don's Regiment transferred to Camp
Shanks, New York at which time he learned they were going
to be deployed to Europe, not the Pacific. They were issued
new uniforms suitable for fighting in Europe. If there was
any good news it was the fact that they would not be fighting
in the water. Don boarded the USS James Parker, which was
the Flagship of a 100 Ship convoy crossing the Atlantic. On

board there were 4,000 paratroopers. In his sleeping quarters he only had a hammock. To avoid being sunk by German submarines they zigzagged across the Atlantic Ocean which took 11 days before docking at Belfast, Ireland. They arrived in early January, 1944. For the next four weeks they endured strenuous training for combat in Germany. In February,1944 they were transferred to Wollaton Park, Nottingham England. They remained in Nottingham until June 1944 when they were shipped to Langley Air Force Base in England and at that time officially became a part of the 82nd Airborne Division which was going to fight in Normandy. At Langley they practiced nighttime jumps and prepared all their gear and resources to make the assault at Normandy successful.

D-Day – June 6, 1944

Men waiting in the hangers at Langley were ready to go. Tension ran high, as the men were anxious to move along. Every effort was made by the commanding officers and non-coms to keep the men at ease. It was not easy. There were accidents from men toying with hand grenades, cleaning their rifles, and pistols. Incredibly a live grenade was thrown from a hanger when a trooper couldn't get the pin back in. Another trooper was shot through the mouth when his buddy pulled the trigger on his rifle and lodged a few rounds through the roof of the hanger. They were more than ready to leave Langley. They were well-trained paratroopers, but waiting was enough to make them mad. On the evening of June 5th, Red Cross Girls handed out coffee and donuts. Most of the men were gorging themselves for they did not know when they would ever enjoy such treats again.

General Matthew Ridgway, Commanding General of the 82nd Airborne Division predicted that 85% of the Paratroopers invading Normandy would be lost in battle. (Unbelievable)

The Troopers boarded the C – 47's to carry them across the channel to Normandy. As Don remembers, the night was clear with only a few clouds. As they moved over the English Channel, with the throbbing engines beating a tattoo in their heads, Don had time to think, what am I doing here(?), what am I about to encounter(?), could I really shoot someone(?), said this young farm boy from a peaceful Village in Ohio. With all those Germans waiting for me will the invasion be successful? Will all of us accomplish our missions? Will any of us see home again? So many questions, and he knew the answers lie ahead of them-- somewhere in Normandy. The

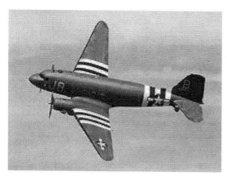 bouncing and motion of the plane was beginning to make their stomachs churn with all the coffee and donuts which made many sick as hell. Then, as they were nearing the Normandy coast they heard and felt the explosion of flak shaking their airplane.

Don returned to his seat and no sooner had he sat down up came all the coffee and donuts. He didn't make too many friends on that flight, as it helped many more to become air sick.

Don forgot he was sick as the command "stand up and hook up" came loud and clear from their jump master. Next, the familiar "sound off for equipment check", 16 okay, 14 okay, etc. They stood waiting. Then came the green light and the command "let's go men, good luck".

A total of 12,000 paratroopers were deployed at Normandy. Their mission was to set up roadblocks and keep the Germans away from the beaches of Normandy.

They Jumped! They were out in the darkness, their chutes opened with a jolt, and the paratroopers were on their way down into the unknown. Don could see a burning village, which he found out later was Sainte-Mere-Eglise. Slowly, he floated downward and landed in the branches of a tree in a small church yard. He was "all shook up". It was not a healthy place to land as the Germans would have the clear advantage. He used his trench knife to cut free of his harness and dropped to the ground, about 10 feet from where he was hanging. He made a dash for the nearest hedgerow and huddled down. The paratroopers had been issued crickets (a kid's plaything) to use in identifying one another in the dark. Don decided he was never going to sit there and click that thing to give away his position. He threw it away. He waited for what seemed ages before he began to realize that he was alone, in Normandy, not knowing the whereabouts of his fellow paratroopers. It was now 1:20 AM June 6, 1944.
For the next four days Don played hide and seek with the jerries (German Soldiers). To his great relief, he came across some troopers of the 101st and was glad to see them. For the next few days he was on a number of patrols, but making every effort to locate his outfit. On the 10th day, he finally reached the H company area. He was home with his squad, his platoon, his company.

NORMANDY – July 4, 1944

The day started with a slight fog and mist. It was always cold in the early morning hours of those days in Normandy. For some reason it was even colder, or at least they imagined it. On this particular morning, H company and the 508 Regiment prepared for an offensive against a strong fortified hillside. The approach to the hill was fronted by a field. It seemed much bigger than most fields. All fields in the area were always surrounded by hedgerows. H company led the frontal attack and began moving out into the field.

Almost immediately mortar and machine-gun fire began to pour into their ranks. They then realized they were in a German mine field. Explosions, screams of, "I'm hit", echoed across the field. Don began to run straight down the field, not toward the hill. He continued to run and was frustrated by the slowness of his feet. How he managed to survive the crossing of the field, he will never know but he is not ashamed to admit that he was praying to God on every step that he took. Afraid? You can bet on it.

He finally reached the hedgerow at the end of the field. He was out of breath and it took a few minutes to realize that he was all alone. Peering beyond the hedgerow he could see four fellow paratroopers lying in a crumpled heap, their bodies torn apart by machine gun bullets. He later learned that over 30 men of H Company were either killed or wounded in the attack across the field.

As he lay hidden in the hedgerow, he could see the German weapons still firing. Don zeroed in on a machine gun nest and emptied his clip of his M-1. Suddenly it became deathly still. No firing, no sounding of birds, only some rustling of tree branches overhead. He noticed a steep bank, about 20 or 30 feet high. He knew that he had to move in that direction to try to find his way back to his original position. It took some hard convincing of his inner- fear, knowing that he had to climb that bank in full view of any Germans who may still be nearby. There was a cold sweat all over his body. He admitted he was scared, but not too scared to just lay there and possibly be shot or captured. He made a mad dash for that bank, and succeeded in getting over it without getting shot. He slid down the other side directly into a drainage ditch. As he moved about 50 yards along the ditch, he noticed a trooper sitting with his back against the bank. The trooper had been wounded and could not walk. He told the trooper that they both had to move along. Don was amazed when the trooper would not let him take him back to camp.

To this day, it haunts Don that he had to leave his comrade behind. He often has wondered how he made out, because even though Don did eventually find his way back to the lines, and told the medics about this man, he never saw him again. During the Normandy Campaign this was Don's lowest point in battle.

After his return that day, Don learned that the hill was covered with a Hitler Youth Division. These young fanatics fought fiercely. He later was to learn that the entire German Division was soon wiped out. Of all the fighting he had encountered in those days of Normandy, none left an everlasting impression as did July 4, 1944, a day of death and destruction!

On July 13, 1944 Donald's regiment was evacuated to England. He had spent 37 days in combat. Out of 12,000 paratroopers who landed at Normandy only 3,200 got back to England.

Holland-September 17, 1944

After Normandy, returning to Wollaton Park, in England training became very serious for those veterans who had survived their first test in combat. They received replacements to fill the vacated spots of their missing comrades. The caliber of the new men was very good. They seemed to be eager to learn, and trained hard. They listened intently to the stories and experiences the Normandy veterans related about the German soldier's ability to fight as well as their methods. They were anxious to know about the famous German 88 and the rapid- fire machine guns. They had been told stories about those damn 88's and they were assured that the stories were true. Don received a promotion to squad leader in the third platoon; the same squad that he had started with at Blanding, Florida.

The months of July, August and the first part of September past quickly. They knew that they would be called upon once again for combat duties. It finally came on Sunday, September 17, 1944. On a bright sunny day, they loaded into the C-47 that was to carry them across the Channel to Holland. The trip was almost uneventful. However, upon approaching their drop zone, the plane was hit by flak, with the right engine on fire. The jump master calmly gave the order to stand up and hook up and stand in the door. Their plane was in a slow descent, and without waiting for a green light, they were still able to clear the plane before it crashed.

They landed in a plowed field, some distance from their assembly area. By evening, Don had gotten together with the rest of his company. The very next day they were involved in a brief firefight. They captured 60 German soldiers. They were at a loss as to what to do with them. They finally located a barn in the middle of a field and herded them into it. They placed one guard in front and back while the rest of their squad stayed close by. Finally, their commanding officer relieved their squad from this duty, but no one knows what ever happened to those 60 German prisoners.

They moved towards Berg en Dal with the objective to capture the Groot Hotel and the town of Beek. Again, they captured a large group of German soldiers. This time they were passed to men who had been assigned to guard prisoners. They dug in around the Groot Hotel, which overlooked Beek and the flats below. They could look out into Germany. Suddenly they began to receive heavy artillery fire, coming from some distance away. The guns had a pattern, one short, one long, the next in the middle. The troopers had learned to recognize enemy artillery for this method of fire. The fight for Beek was indeed a hectic and scary experience.

Battles raged in and out of Beek all night long. The Germans would be driven out, and withdraw back up the hill. It took

four such attacks before H Company of the 508th Parachute Infantry Regiment secured the area.

In this action, they were the first unit to fight on German soil and hold ground.

On September 22, while assembled near their slit trenches near the Groot Hotel, they once again heard the distant boom from the German artillery. They made a mad dash for their trenches as the artillery came crashing down around them. When the shelling stopped, five men had been killed, including an officer and many wounded, including Don. His fellow paratroopers carried him back to the aid station. He had received shrapnel in his leg, back, face and arms. He was indeed lucky to be alive. The helmet he was wearing had a hole directly in the middle of the non—com stripe on the back of it. Don asked to be returned to his squad, but the doctor told him he would need surgery to remove the shrapnel from his legs and back; something they could not do at the aid station. He needed to be transferred to a Divisional Hospital.

Actually, he felt all right, but he realized it was the fact that they had given him something to ease the pain. From the cuts on his head and his face, blood was everywhere, and it looked worse than it really was. Don tells me that he will never forget the hospital where they took him. It was in Nijmegen and had been used as a Hitler baby factory. He was amazed to see hundreds of baby buggies in the basement entry and in the hallways. Regardless, they wasted no time in performing surgery and removing the pieces of shrapnel from his legs, back and arms. He awoke lying in a hallway with many other wounded troopers.

Don recalled being able to see just the very top of the Nijmegen Bridge where he laid. The next day, two German fighter planes strafed and tried to bomb the bridge.

Immediately, an American P– 51 appeared and engaged the two German fighters. In no time one of the German planes came tumbling towards the ground with the pilot bailing out. The American's captured him. As the prisoner passed by their hospital- tent they could see that he was dressed in a black leather suit and looked like he was about 19 or 20 years old. He appeared scared as hell, and they could have cared less. In a few days Don was transferred to another field hospital and it was there that they found a bullet lodged in the back of his head. After the Doctor and Nurse operated to remove the bullet, while resting on a stretcher, a second German fighter plane began to strafe the hospital. He couldn't believe it possible, but the doctor and nurse who had just operated on him were still working in the same operating room, at the same operating table, and were killed instantly.

Don was moved the next day to yet another field hospital. Eventually, he was evacuated from Brussels to a hospital in Oxford, England. It was a short stay before he was transferred to another hospital in Coventry. Here, he learned what it means to be bombed. The Germans apparently intended to wipe out this industrial city. Most of Coventry was completely destroyed. He began to wonder if the Germans were looking for him? First the strafing, then the bombing. He just wanted to go home!
His road to recovery took about three months. He returned to Wollaton Park and was told he was being transferred to another outfit. He raised so much hell that they finally agreed to send him back to his own company camped at Sissone, France. He arrived on the night of December 15, 1944 just in

time to get his squad back and ride those trucks into the Ardennes.

THE BATTLE OF THE BULGE (THE ARDENNES CAMPAIGN)

Everything seemed to be going along peacefully for the Division while in Sissone, France. They had just finished a tough campaign in Holland. Their Division was reorganizing the troops, letting them catch up on some rest and relaxation. They were also receiving badly needed replacements. Many troopers were straggling in from various hospitals in England, where they had been recovering from wounds received in Holland. On December 17, an alert was sounded for all commanding officers and their staff to report to their perspective areas. Notice was announced to all enlisted men to return to their companies. A rumble of excitement existed throughout their camp. Orders were given to assemble all gear ready as Division was making preparations to move out to the front lines. Rumor had it that Germans had made a breakthrough and the Division was needed immediately to help stem the tide of the German offensive. This action was taking place somewhere in Belgium called the Ardennes.

They were not sure if they were to jump into combat as they did in Normandy and Holland, but they soon learned the answer. All night, trucks could be heard rumbling throughout the camp. New weapons were being issued to everyone, still packed in Cosmoline, the protective grease used to ship weapons overseas. Gasoline rations were immediately provided and the cleaning of these weapons was a priority. Working throughout the night, equipment was made ready. Early on the morning of December 18, 1944 orders came to load onto large cattle trucks, with standing room only. Their ride into Belgium lasted twenty hours in twenty below zero weather. It was an experience to remember and hate. However, it certainly beat having to make a parachute drop into that wild conflict. Even with all the fighting, the freezing weather, short food rations, and the lack of warm clothing, if you ask a veteran of those days, he will first tell you about that damn truck ride into the Ardennes.

They had been moving and fighting continuously throughout the first few days in the Ardennes. From the time they off – loaded the trucks until January 31, 1945 H Company was constantly on the front lines. Moving, fighting, digging foxholes, fighting the bitter cold and the frostbitten feet, begging for rest and some sleep, hoping for hot chow, but getting none. It was mind-boggling to say the least. It was a test for even the strong-willed paratroopers.

In Dons' words-------"Moving towards the Municipality of St. Vith there had been fierce fighting. Three tanks of ours were suddenly under fire from a German "modified 88 Gun" King Tiger Tank. We flattened ourselves close to the ground as the shells whistled over our heads. The rounds were coming from above us on a snow- covered bridge. All three American tanks burst into flames when the 88's hit. The American crewmen tried to struggle free of their tanks, but were engulfed in flames. It was a horrendous thing to see. All the crews gave of their lives. We moved quickly towards the area where the 88's were coming. The Tiger tank was stuck in a trench and was unable to free itself. In a brisk fight, we overran the tank, capturing 17 prisoners. It was very difficult to keep from killing the men who had just wiped out so many of our comrades. These prisoners were tough looking and rugged veterans. We were fortunate, because although paratroopers were fighters, we were not murderers and could not kill prisoners once they were unarmed. Not since Normandy had unarmed prisoners been shot".

On Christmas morning, the Troopers remained in defensive positions. Looking down a slope through a group of trees, they saw a yellow house with chickens in the barnyard. It was like an invitation to dinner.

Without hesitation, Don took two men and marched down the slope to the house. Inside they found some potatoes. It was decided that they were going to celebrate Christmas. They caught a chicken, peeled some potatoes and started a fire in the small wood burning stove. A stupid mistake on the Paratrooper's part because the Germans saw the smoke coming from the chimney. They were cooking the chicken and potatoes when suddenly they heard the screeching and screening of an 88 mm mortar heading their way. They hastily made a beeline away from the house and seconds later the house was incinerated. To make things worse that afternoon they were in another small house and barn, and once again artillery began to fall. They all made a mad scramble for their foxholes but Don found himself with a problem. Still in the house, an 88 hit the dwelling bringing the entire roof and barn down on top of him. If it had not been for a slit trench behind the cows, he would have perished. Fortunately, no cows had passed that way recently. He could hear his men calling, "hey Sarge," you all right?" Hell, no he wasn't, but he was alive. They dug him out of that mess, but he thinks one or two thought they should leave him there. What a Christmas it had been-- no chicken. In retrospect those K rations tasted pretty good after all. Just being alive to eat them was very satisfying.

On January 31, 1945 the 82nd Airborne was sent to the town of Werbomont to shield against a German attack. This occurred during the closing days of the Ardennes Offensive. Don was shot through the lung by a German sniper. He was carried to an aid station by two German prisoners and loaded into an ambulance for the trip to the Division Hospital at Leige. During the trip the driver lost control of the ambulance and it rolled over and over down the side of a mountain landing upside down in a river. Everyone was killed except Don. He was rescued when American soldiers spotted the wreckage. Don recovered and was released on August 25, 1945 from Memphis General Hospital, USA.

After the war, in 1946, Don married his beautiful wife Roselyn. They have four children --Don, Kim, David and Denise. They also have six grandchildren and seven great-grandchildren. Don enjoyed many years in the business world as a CPA and Director of International Sales for a large manufacturing company. He also takes an active interest in local community affairs around Johnstown, Ohio.

MEDALS AND DECORATIONS

- PARACHUTE WINGS
- BRONZE ARROW HEAD
- COMBAT STARS (2)
- PURPLE HEART WITH CLUSTER
- BRONZE STARS (4)
- FOUR COMBAT BATTLE STARS
- COMBAT INFANTRY BADGE
- PRESIDENTIAL CITATION
- VICTORY MEDAL
- GOOD CONDUCT MEDAL
- FRENCH FOURRAGERRE CROIX DE GERRE
- ORANGE LANYARD HOLLAND

- BELGIUM FOURRAGERE
- EUROPEAN THEATER MEDAL
- OVERSEAS CHEVRONS (3)

FOREIGN AWARDS

- FRENCH MEDAL OF HONOR
- FRENCH D- DAY MEDAL
- FIRST ALLIED ARMY PATCH (USA-BRITISH-FRENCH- POLISH)

Don also is a member of the Ohio Veterans Hall of Fame and Ford Oval of Honor

DON JAKEWAY – THANK YOU FOR YOUR SERVICE

Fred Zacharias

(This complete story is taken from "From the Trenches",
Published in Fall, 2016 by Colonel L. Albers, USAF, Ret. and
provided by Motts Military Museum)

One has to be incredibly impressed with all that Fred, nick
name Zack, Zacharias experienced during his first 21 years.
We have all heard stories about the Greatest Generation and
what they endured during the Great Depression and World
War II to complete their lives happily and successfully. Fred
Zacharias is a perfect example.

Fred was born on July 29, 1925. His hometown of Wellsville,
Ohio in north eastern, Ohio was considered a part of
Appalachia; not an affluent region in the best of times. The
two largest industries in the area were potteries and steel
mills, and both, along with other businesses, were forced to
close and layoff their employees during the great depression
of the 1930s. Fred's dad was a steelworker and among those

who lost his job. The family rented half of a three-story house in Wellsville with no electricity. Lighting was by gas lamps and heating was from a single, large coal stove in the middle of the living room. They did have a cow, chickens, and pigs to assist with the family's food supply; but they were also eligible for relief. Fred recalls visiting the relief office for flour, sugar, dried beans, and canned meat to supplement seasonal produce from a small garden.

Fred loved reading, truly enjoyed school, and was fortunate enough to have some dedicated, caring teachers to encourage and mentor him. He had some vision problems and had to wear glasses from a young age. He was left – handed and fondly remembers the teacher who taught him a method to write that way rather than forcing him to write right – handed.

His grade school years were spent in a one- room school. Fred was pleased that his last name began with a "Z". Having students seated alphabetically caused them to be seated in the back of the room, which was near the stove – a blessing in the winter. During those years, he was forced to walk two miles each way to school. When he entered sixth grade, it was a middle school comprised of grades six, seven, and eight – a much larger school with students coming from other elementary schools in the area. Unfortunately, Fred had to walk four miles each way to school during this period.

1939 was a pivotal year for the Zacharias family. Fred's father had become an alcoholic, and the family was in chaos. Fred's grandmother offered to give his dad $1,000 to buy a local farm, which he did – $750 as a down payment on the farm and $250 to purchase a team of workhorses. Their "new" home was a two-story, four rooms with no gas, running water, or electricity. Water had to be carried from a well about 50 yards for home usage, and the bathroom was also a good distance from the house – a two-hole outhouse. Fred did his homework by kerosene lantern at the kitchen table. Since they were now out of the city limits of Wellsville, at least he was allowed to ride the bus to school and back, a real blessing. After two years in this house they finally got electricity and bought a refrigerator.

Family farming was hard work, because everything was done by hand or using horses – but they were able to raise enough food for the family and also various items to sell in town. By the time Fred was in eighth grade, he had two brothers and a sister; but they were too young to be of much help with the numerous chores. The end of eighth grade was a turning point in young Fred's life. Since the family was barely eking out a living, it was impossible to hire extra workers to run the farm. It was common in those days for young men to quit school after eighth grade to work full – time on the farm. (In fact, that's what happened to Fred's three younger brothers when they reached that age). There were some heated family discussions on the matter, but Fred's mother sternly told his father that, "if Freddie wants to go to high school, then he will go." His mom's decision and statement were key to Fred's later scholastic achievements.

Farm life was extremely difficult for the family. Daily chores included milking the cows, feeding all the animals, fixing fences, planting, harvesting, and caring for the horses... Among other tasks. Ultimately, Fred became responsible for the five or six horses. Before leaving for school, Fred had to harness them for work. When he returned from school, he had to feed them, curry and brush them, take care of any injuries they had, put them out to pasture, clean out their stalls, and replenish them with clean straw. It was hard, time – consuming labor.

Fred never planned upon continuing education beyond high school, so he just took general courses. He has always been pleased that he took a typing course, because his skill at a keyboard has become a vital asset used daily later in life. Graduating high school in May, 1943 Fred turned 18, and two months later registered for the draft. About the same-time he did try to enlist in the Navy V – 12 Program but was turned down due to bad teeth. As soon as he graduated, Fred took a temporary job in the steel mill, where he worked various jobs for only a couple of months before receiving orders to report to an induction center in Cleveland, Ohio. He was transported by bus to the processing center for military physical and mental examinations. At the end of the day he was ushered into a room with representatives of the various military branches, where Fred could choose which branch he wanted.

He selected and was accepted into the US Marine Corps. On November 9, 1943, Fred Zacharias signed on the dotted line to serve as a Marine for the duration of the war.

Not long after, Fred received orders to report to Parris Island, South Carolina for induction and boot camp. For a young lad who had never been more than 50 miles from home, this was an experience indeed! After taking a bus to Pittsburgh, he took trains to Washington DC and several other stops before being loaded on a semi – truck with cattle car siding and no seats to be driven to Parris Island. Drill instructors ordered them to strip naked and put their civilian clothes in bags to be shipped home later. The next stop was at the barbershop, where each recruit was cut bald. Next, they showered. After drying off, the men went through a variety of physical exams and shots.

Next, they were paraded through the clothing area, where each man received his allotment of military clothing. The final stop was where they were issued boots,vital to all the walking and marching facing them for the next nine weeks. (in combat during World War II, Marines wore only boots). Finally, that day, they were marched to barracks and endlessly briefed on rules and schedules before selecting a bunk and footlocker in the barracks that was their new home.

Throughout Boot Camp, the platoons marched everywhere. Each man was issued a M1 rifle and learned to disassemble and reassemble it blindfolded. Although forced to shoot right – handed, Fred shot expert rifleman, raising his monthly salary by five dollars. Of course, the recruits had endless classes on military discipline and courtesy, health, personal hygiene, bayonet usage, gas mask drills, and numerous other topics. In one class, the men were subjected to two sounds and asked if they were the same or different. Because Fred did so well on those tasks, he was fortunate enough to be selected for the communications field rather than directly into a combat platoon.

With a sigh of relief, Fred left Parris Island and returned home to Wellsville for a ten- day leave. He was proud to show friends and family his Marine green uniform with the expert rifleman badge on his chest and one red stripe on each sleeve – Private First Class.

At the completion of his leave Pfc. Zacharias traveled again by train to Camp Lejeune, North Carolina, for his new schooling to become a radio operator. At first, the training consisted of sitting at a table wearing earphones while listening to and writing down five – letter groups of letters sent in Morse code. Obviously, 7 ½ hours of this per day was incredibly boring and monotonous, but they had to perfect this skill to graduate. The only diversion was when they got to actually use a telegraph key to send Morse code messages. Once they mastered that, his platoon was able to go back to a daytime schedule for the rest of the communications training, a huge relief. Of course, physical fitness is a big part of Marine training; and that meant countless hours of marching and exercising each week. The frequent marches entailed carrying a backpack or radio on their backs at forced march speeds during these five- or ten-mile jaunts. They also had to run an obstacle course several times a week.

Following this four-month school again the USMC decided what to do with each graduate. While most of Fred's classmates were sent to Camp Pendleton, California for combat training, Fred was one of the few selected to attend basic radio repair school in downtown Omaha Nebraska. Among other things, trainees were given a box of parts and required to build their own receiver. They also were given broken radios and required to figure out what was needed to fix them. Usually this was the determining the broken part and replacing it, which enabled Fred to become very proficient with a soldering iron. The group was proud impressing the locals as they marched together to and from class.

Next, Fred was transported by train to Camp Pendleton for additional training in a combat environment. He was assigned to a telephone unit and taught how to set up and operate switchboards into trouble – shoot disrupted telephone lines. This often happened in the dark of night; and, simulating combat conditions, the trainees were not allowed to use lighting to find and repair the simulated problem. On August 27, 1944 the 27th Marine Regiment sailed from San Diego to a new home on the big Island of Hawaii called Camp Tarawa. There they trained on beach landings and began to stockpile equipment and supplies for an upcoming invasion. Fred's unit, the 27th Replacement Battalion remained at Camp Pendleton, until they sailed from San Diego to Hilo on Thanksgiving Day. Not having "sea legs," Fred immediately became quite ill and could not **leave his bunk.**

When Fred's unit landed at Hilo, it was taken by railroad flat car to Hanokaa and then by truck to Camp Tarawa. After getting settled in a tent, the Marines spent many days loading and unloading trucks of invasion supplies. Soon, however, the communication personnel were exempt from all work details, as they began working 24 – hour shifts. At the end of  December ships were loaded, and they departed for Pearl Harbor to join a huge convoy formation. That would be their home until the day of the invasion. Fred's unit, the 27th Replacement was quartered on the USS Cecil along with several other units. Their job would be to unload the ships at the invasion landing area. For the next month the ships took up invasion formations for practice landings on the island of Maui. Each time, once the practice rehearsals were over, they would return to Pearl Harbor to refuel and re-supply.

Finally, on January 27, 1945, the vast convoy left Pearl Harbor and headed west across the Pacific. The Marines still do not know their destination. Aboard the ship, the Marines could look over the rails and marvel at the huge number of ships. As far as one could see, there were ships everywhere. Two days out of Hawaii, the Marines of the 5th Division were finally informed of their destination, **Iwo Jima. It was a small island, 5 miles wide and 8 miles long – located about 700 miles south of the Japanese home islands. This would be the first area owned by the Japanese prior to the war that would be attacked by US forces.**

The Pacific command felt the Iwo Jima invasion would be only a three to five- day operation in length and the Iwo Jima units could move on and be back up for the pending Okinawa invasion. Unfortunately, they had no idea how fortified the island was – with a vast tunnel system and other fortifications that stood up to the previous nine months of bombardment by Naval and Air Corps  Units. The actual battle lasted from February 19 to March 23.

During the first 48 hours of the invasion the Navajo code talkers (wind talkers) did all the communications between the beach and the invasion ships. They performed the task flawlessly. On the third day of the invasion Fred received orders to pack his gear and go ashore to join HQ, first Battalion, 27th Marine Regiment. Normally, a headquarters is a mile or so away from the front lines; but, because the island was so small, it was less than 100 yards from the front- line action. Therefore, it was under constant mortar attack. Flames generally lit up the entire area all night, every night. Against heavy enemy fire, the Marines fought northward, sometimes gaining a few yards a day. **Mount Suribachi did not have a fortified tunnel system; and on the fifth day of the invasion Fred witnessed the Marines of the 28th Regiment raise the American flag there.**

In early March, Fred was designated to take a new radio to the front and bring back a damaged one. A Japanese soldier in a spider hole took a shot at him. Fortunately, it hit the radio that he was carrying on his back, which may have saved his life. He called for help, and soon the Japanese soldier was killed by another Marine. From that time forward, those 40-pound radios carried on his back never seemed heavy. Fred appreciated the protection they provided.

While all of his combat experiences, one aspect always intrigued Fred and continued to pop into his mind. The regimental chaplain, Lieut. Louis Valbracht, on numerous occasions, totally unarmed exposed himself in the middle of the battlefield giving comfort to an injured or dying Marine. Fred pondered what would motivate a man to take such risks. The Chaplin was an enigma to Fred and it became a prevailing mystery to him. Slowly it dawned on Fred that it must have been the chaplain's faith that enabled him to perform these acts of kindness and courage.

On March 23, 1945, Fred's battalion left Iwo Jima on a landing craft headed for ships that would take them back to the 5th Division camp on the big Island of Hawaii. Just before boarding, Fred attended a religious service held by the chaplain. To this day, Fred recalls the chaplain asking, "why are you alive today?" Then, with lots of tears they sang the Navy Hymn, "Eternal Father, Strong to Save".

Fred's Battalion arrived on the beaches of Iwo Jima with 1,000 Marines and Sailors. They departed with only 210

who had not been killed or wounded.

Back at Camp Tarawa they continued their drills preparing for the next invasion, Japan itself – probably Okinawa. One morning Fred was ordered to report to the commanding officer, Maj. Russell. Fred was informed that he was relieved of his normal communications duties and would become Russell's personal radioman. The job came with a major perk. He was able to ride in a Jeep with the major, rather than marching everywhere like the other Marines. The bad news was that in combat, he would be a sitting duck, seated in a Jeep with a big radio on his back and a big antenna sticking in the air. The enemy would certainly know where to shoot. **And then it happened-on August 6th and 9th, the atomic bombs were dropped on Hiroshima and Nagasaki.** On August 16, the Japanese announced they were surrendering to the Allies. Instead of another invasion and more combat, the 5th Marine Division was to become an occupying force in Japan. In mid – September 1945 Fred's regiment boarded ships at Hilo and set sail for the port city of Sasebo on the island of Kyushu.

 The headquarters for the 5th Marine Division was set up at the former Japanese Naval Training Center at Ainoura. There they set up their regimental radio system, mainly to keep in contact with ships out in the harbor. Soon they were granted passes to travel and sightsee around the area. For Fred, his most dramatic trip was to visit the city of Nagasaki; and, to this day, he vividly recalls the total annihilation of everything from buildings to vegetation. Fred remained on occupation duty on Kyushu from September 1945 until June 1946, at which time he had finally accumulated enough combat points and overseas duties to make him eligible to return home to the United States.

Upon arrival at Pearl Harbor it was all hands-on deck, and the troops stood at attention and saluted as they passed the sunken USS Arizona. It was an extremely emotional event for all board. The next stop was at Panama City. Sailing up the Atlantic Coast, they finally landed at the huge Navy port of Norfolk, Virginia. The Marines were loaded aboard buses and driven to the Marine base at Quantico, Virginia, to be discharged. The discharge process took a number of days. As Fred was being read his record, it was the first time he learned that he had been promoted to corporal. And,

furthermore, if he volunteered to reenlist, he would be promoted on the spot to Sgt. **Fred politely declined the offer.**

He was more than ready to be a civilian once again. He was a very different person now, and this farm boy had grown into a man. To this day, Fred is proud to say, **"I will always be a Marine."** He certainly has a memory bank filled even today with experiences few will ever encounter. But since leaving Iwo Jima, there has always been one memory still very much alive and active to this day. That is the memory of the Chaplain on his last day in the service asking the question, "why are you alive today?"

LIFE AND THE WAR EXPERIENCE

Upon returning to the farm, nobody in his family seemed to want to know much about what Fred experienced as a Marine. He simply went back to working the farm and got on with his life as before. Fred started attending church and began building a quest for a faith foundation. Soon, he decided that he wanted to become a minister.

Using the G.I. Bill, Fred attended Hiram College in Hiram, Ohio, a private Protestant College and earned his BA in 1952. In 1956, Fred graduated from Oberlin Graduate School of Theology with a Bachelor of Divinity degree. In 1974 Fred earned his Dr. of Ministry Degree from Vanderbilt University in Nashville. Before retiring and moving to Columbus to be close to his daughter. Fred served as a parish minister in Ohio and then California. He is eternally grateful for the Lord's leading him through his life of faith and service.

Looking back upon his life Fred is 100% convinced that serving in the Marine Corps is the best thing that ever happened to him. Being a Marine changed his life in many ways.

Discipline: The practice of training people to obey rules or codes of behavior, using punishment to correct disobedience.

Perseverance: Steadfastness in doing something despite the difficulty or delay in achieving success.

Teamwork: the combined action of a group of people, especially when effective and efficient.

Today, Fred lives in his apartment in a retirement village and has many close friends who he has very deep respect for both emotionally and spiritually. He can joke, tease and harass others in a caring and loving attitude. He loves them and they love him.

When Fred wakes up each morning, he makes a conscious decision to decide what to do with his life this day. **The first thing he does each day ---He makes his bed!!!**

Fred has experienced the ravages of the Great Depression of the 1930s, fighting as a Marine on Iwo Jima, attending college and becoming an ordained minister and even recovering from brain surgery. **What a fulfilling life!**

My final question to Fred is the same question the chaplain asked him when he was discharged from the Marine Corps

"Why are you alive today?"
Fred's answer – "To be the person I am today"

Fred E. Zacharias – THANK YOU FOR YOUR SERVICE

Daniel A. Carmichael Jr.

In 1936, Danny Carmichael graduated from the Columbus Academy in Columbus, Ohio. A brilliant student became a football, basketball, baseball and golf legend. He is the first recipient of the Academy's Athletic Hall of Fame and to this day, he is probably the most outstanding athlete ever to graduate from this private school dating back to 1911.

In 1941, he received his diploma from Princeton University in the School of Architecture with Honors. He was a three-year baseball player and was captain and twice an all-league basketball star. It appeared that he was destined to be a success in life. The predictions proved to be correct!

In the spring of 1941 Dan went to the recruiting station at the old post office building in downtown Columbus to enlist. At the time he had no preference about which service to enter. When his turn came for his physical- exam he took the X – Ray pictures of his knees, which had been badly injured in freshman football, and gave them to the medical officer in charge. Dan didn't think the doctor
had the faintest idea of what he was looking at. He simply said "you're 4F" (exempt from service). In the spring of 1941 that was fine with him. This all occurred nine months before Pearl Harbor.
Pearl Harbor changed all that, and like millions of others he wanted to enlist and be a part of the Armed Forces. Dan had always been fascinated by airplanes. Growing up, all the model airplanes that he built were fighter planes.

Months later back at the old post office recruiting station he changed his tactics. This time he went to the Navy Air Corps recruiting station and said that he wanted to enlist in the Navy Air Corps but was worried about his draft classification. The recruiter, thinking that he was 1A and worried about him being drafted said "pass your physical exam and you are ours". In later times he was warned that he might have trouble with nitrogen bubbles in his knees in high – speed dives, but he never had the slightest difficulty.

Dan graduated from Pensacola on March 14, 1943 with a pair of Gold Wings and Ensign Bars.

Dan, as a newly commissioned Ensign, was stationed at NAS Opa Locka, Florida for 30 days of advanced operational fighter training to be followed by carrier landing qualification on the U.S.S. Card. After Dan made the grade, he was assigned to a fleet squadron.

World War II Combat Naval Aviator

In late 1943 Air Group 2(VF2 fighters, VB2 dive bombers, VT2 torpedo bombers) was operating at Naval Air Station Quonset Point, Rhode Island, waiting for orders to go to the Pacific. In early October they  received their orders. They flew their 36 VF planes across the country (two days) and were transported via a CVE (small carrier) to Hawaii.

They had been headed for Guadalcanal, but were not needed there by the time they reached Hawaii. After a few weeks at Naval Air Station Barbers Point they (VF2) were suddenly assigned to Air Group 6 on the USS Enterprise for the invasion of Tarawa. Fighter squadron VF6 was detached and sent ashore. They must have done something terrible.

Dan's Air Group was one of the largest yet assembled. Their Air Group commander was Lieut. Cmdr. EH (Butch) O'Hare, one of the Navy's early heroes and holder of the Congressional Medal of Honor. The task force was, without doubt, the largest yet put together. Eventually it included aircraft Carriers Enterprise, Yorktown Lexington, Bunker Hill, Essex, Independence, Saratoga, Princeton, Cowpens, Monterey, and the Belleau Wood along with four battleships and the appropriate mix of cruisers and destroyers. The "flag" for their group, Rear Adm. Radford, was on the Enterprise.

During the nine days in route from Pearl Harbor to the Gilbert Islands (Tarawa) routine flight operations were conducted. Lieut. Cmdr. O'Hare was very much a part of such operations. Dan was an Ensign and O'Hare was his air group commander, but he enjoyed his presence and Dan listened whenever he could. On November 20th, all carrier aircraft flew the usual bombing and strafing attacks against assigned targets in preparation for and in support of the landing forces. The invasion proceeded on schedule, and the bitter battle that developed has been well described.

During this time, almost every night there were enemy bombers that passed "nearby" the fleet on their way to attack our forces at Tarawa just before dawn.

For some reason or another, they made no effort to attack the fleet. On November 23rd Lieut. Cmdr. O'Hare decided to lead a four- plane division early the next morning in an attempt to intercept the group of 25 to 30 bombers passing them each night. They encountered no enemy planes.

On the night of November 24th, shortly after dark their situation changed dramatically. The enemy bombers did not pass "nearby" but instead came after the fleet. At about 2100 (9:00 P.M.) "general quarters" was sounded and reports of "many bogies" were received one after another. Later estimates ranged from 30 to 40 enemy bombers roaming around and within the task groups.

Their ships were constantly maneuvering violently to avoid attack, imagined or real, and also frequently to seek the cover provided by low storm clouds in the area. Dan knew nothing about ships or boats or how they handled, and he was totally unprepared for the big Enterprises evasive maneuvers. When the ship went into what they call a "full rudder" turn the flight deck pitched to an angle that absolutely convinced Dan it was going to roll over. He was ready to jump at a moment's notice, not just the first time, but every time it happened.

Every so often, apparently on command of radar controllers, the whole fleet would open up with all anti–aircraft weapons. Dan had never seen a 4th of July display to even come close to that site. Thousands of tracers in every direction with the accompanying noise was something that he never experienced again.

The following night was pretty much a repeat of the same activity with the addition of many flares being dropped as the enemy bombers attempted to locate individual ships for an attack. None of the American ships were hit, but it seemed only a matter of time if this action continued. Something had to be done.

The solution was that commander O'Hare and his wing man be launched about dusk, and with the use of the torpedo squadron skipper, their radar unit might locate enemy aircraft and then be able to visually close to firing range.

The idea was as novel as it was challenging. It would be the first time the Navy ever conducted a carrier –

based night intercept mission. On November 26, shortly after 1900, three planes were launched and headed for their rendezvous point.

Blow-by-blow description over the squawk box
"A large group of bogies on our Port side, 30 miles, closing fast – now it's 17 miles and breaking up into smaller groups – now fanning out – another group to starboard closing fast – O'Hare is closing on a bogie – shot down a Betty – flares are being dropped at 3 miles, all along our starboard – bogies now on all sides, bogies to port closing fast – 3 miles – 5000 yards".

At this point the fleet opened up with the same incredible display of firepower as before – 20 to 30 flares burning at all times to silhouette the fleet. Shrapnel was falling everywhere. The enemy was apparently confused by this unexpected night intercept and related activity and at times were reported to be firing at one another. In confusion they soon withdrew.

When last seen, Lieut. Cmdr. O'Hare had slid out of formation and apparently plunged into the sea. The official conclusion, as reported to them, was that O'Hare was "probably shot down by an enemy plane that joined on the formation".

The efforts of the three pilots from the Enterprise did not go without recognition and appreciation. They were credited with disrupting the largest night attack in Naval Aviation History, but the cost was a terrible price to pay. The Admirals Staff recommended Lieutenant Commander O'Hare for a second Congressional Medal of Honor but the review board reduced it to a Navy Cross.

Lieutenant Commander O'Hare was a fine pilot and an outstanding leader with a brilliant future. To have one of the great airports (Chicago O'Hare) of the world named in his honor is a fitting tribute to this genuine American hero. Dan Carmichael witnessed one - of the greatest Air Corps and Naval maneuvers in American history.

RESCUE AT TRUK

In late April 1944 the fleet spent two days attacking the Japanese bastion of Truk, extensively developed and heavily defended. Dan was a part of the first fighter sweep at dawn. Almost immediately they encountered some enemy fire. He had a beautiful position on two Japanese aircraft when his gunsight failed. Before he could adjust for his tracer fire the enemy slipped into a cloud and he never saw them again.

Dan and his wing man became separated from their commander but they picked up two other planes which enabled them to strafe enemy positions with a full division of four planes. Starting back to his ship, the Hornet, he flew over the main entrance to the harbor and immediately saw a yellow life raft with three people in it. It was some of his fleet people, waving their arms. At the same- time he witnessed several enemy high - speed Motor torpedo boats heading for that raft. Dan immediately began to strafe those boats in an effort to drive them back to the shore. The Japanese had 20 mm cannons and fought them "tooth and toenail". The enemy was tough and brave. Dan estimates that there were about eight or ten boats, half of which were destroyed with the other half heading back to shore and their base. Continuing to fly over the life raft, he then called for a rescue operation. Usually, the rescue service involved a submarine or two, stationed along their flight path to and from the target area. Submarines could not afford to try a rescue in the limited space available so close to shore gunfire. Dan was able to contact a rescue plane that was operating in their area. It was an OS2U Scout seaplane from one of the battleships nearby.

Dan caught sight of the plane about 15 minutes later and could not believe his eyes. There were at least seven or eight pilots/crew on the wings of that airplane. The plane was too heavy to take off so it just "taxied" on the water as best it could. The plane received some gunfire from shore, but it was quickly suppressed. The rescue was quickly completed. The plane "taxied" out to sea to a destroyer waiting at a safe distance, where the "riders" were transferred to the destroyer and then soon taken back to their carriers, and of course, the plane flew back to their battleship home. The pilot of the seaplane just happened to be a close friend and classmate of Dan's at Princeton.

When the OS2U "taxied" up to the destroyer, photos were taken of that plane with people all over its wings. It became one of the most highly publicized pictures of the war.

First battle of the Philippine Sea

On June 20th 1944 their carrier fleet was well west of Guam when the Japanese carrier fleet was cited about 200 miles west of them. They had been waiting all day for such a contact report. Dan and the other pilots immediately launched their fighters, each carrying one 500- pound bomb. They were part of a major fleet attack force of over 200 planes. The launch was at 1600, so there was no chance they would return in daylight. When they were nearing the reported position of the enemy fleet, they were advised that there had been an error in the reported location of the enemy fleet. The error amounted to

100 to 200 miles round-trip. This meant the fighters would be dangerously low on fuel, but for many of the bombers it was obvious they could not reach the fleet on return. They simply didn't have as much range as the fighters.

The strike force was advised that under those circumstances it would be permissible for anyone short of fuel to turn back. Of course, no one did. When they reached the area of the enemy fleet it was growing dark very rapidly. They were flying at about 15,000 feet, and they could find the ships mainly by the wake behind them – and, of course, at the lower altitudes it was even darker.

Commander Dean was leading their group and led them around for a few minutes in search of a prime target. At some point, without any warning he started diving. Dan could just barely make out a large aircraft carrier below them. He turned on his gun sight and armed his bomb, flying close behind and to the side of Dean and his wingmen.

Dan remembers being concerned that they were becoming too steep and too fast for any kind of a decent bombing run. Too steep an angle and having too much speed makes it very difficult to make the corrections that are part of any good bombing run. Suddenly Dean pulled out of the dive. Dan look at his altimeter and it showed they were just below 8000 feet. He felt relieved because he was certain that this had been a step – down dive and that they were now positioning themselves for a good low – altitude dive and release. He was ready because it was growing dark rapidly. However, Dan became concerned because they seemed to be wasting time. To his shock, when he checked his compass, he could not believe his eyes. They were headed back to their fleet. Dan considered breaking away and going back for an attack, but it was now very dark and his fuel was going to be dangerously low on return. He also had his wing man to think about. In total frustration Dan dropped his bomb in the ocean. An absolutely golden opportunity had been wasted by his squadron commander.

The commander led them down into the landing Circle for the USS Hornet. His first pass was a wave – off due to a fouled deck. The next time Dan took a comfortable interval on the plane in front of him, but that plane crashed and instantly became one big ball of fire.

Dan had no choice but to look for another Carrier in order to land safely. He saw a single light in the distance. It was the USS Cabot. He had enough fuel for one Carrier pattern and approach. If he missed for any reason, he would make a power – on water landing beside the ship. No need – he made as good a "pass" as he ever made – "Roger" (perfect) all the way from the landing signal officer.

The next day he was returned to the Hornet. He was greeted by his aircraft intelligence officer who congratulated him on winning the Navy Cross, second only to the Medal of Honor. If a bomb destroys an enemy warship the pilot is automatically awarded a Navy Cross. They said his bomb hit was confirmed. Dan confirmed that "HIS" bomb dropped into the ocean, not on an enemy warship. The intelligence officer replied "you may be the first guy ever to turn down the Navy Cross". It was not in Dan Carmichael's DNA to ever lie.

Iwo Jima

After the Philippine Sea Battle Dan's task group headed north to their favorite hunting grounds, the Bonin Islands (Iwo Jima, Chichi Jima).

On the afternoon of July 3rd, commander Dean led a 60- plane fighter sweep against Iwo Jima, and they had a battle royal against a similar number of enemy planes. It was a wild melee. Dan shot down two and then, as often happens, the sky was suddenly empty – no planes anywhere. His wing man, Nolan Harrigan, was right with him, but Dan had no radio and could not talk to him. His radio control box had been completely destroyed by enemy gunfire.

They had obviously missed their rendezvous area and were low on gas. They took the most direct route straight back to the Hornet, which took them directly over Iwo Jima – a very dumb thing to do.

By manual signals he had Harrigan close on his wing to check on gas and his general condition. Suddenly, Dan's plane was hit by a line of gunfire. Another enemy fighter roared by just above his head and pulled straight up in a vertical climb. A second plane had attacked Harrigan, who broke away to try and throw off his attacker.

Dan was in trouble. His plane was hit in both wing roots, the right wing was on fire, the landing gear was blown out of the wheel wells and was in a "trail" position. The hydraulic system was destroyed and there was oil flowing across the wind screen. The fire control for his guns were destroyed and when he added any significant power the engine was rough.

In all of his flying days two things he enjoyed most were aerobatics and dog – fighting – and that probably saved his life. The enemy pilot was making beautiful overhead high deflection runs on him and he knew exactly what he was doing. Dan needed to delay what seemed to be an inevitable conclusion. When the enemy plane rolled into his dive to make his run, Dan watched his guns – when they fired, he rolled into a hard- tight turn, a turn that the enemy air plane could not match at his high diving speed. The Japanese pilot made a number of runs damaging his left-wing. Japanese and American airplanes have 3 x 50 caliber guns on each wing. The guns are bore – sighted to converge at a point out ahead according to the practice of the squadron- 900 feet, 1000 feet, or even 1200 feet.

When that enemy pilot fired, it gave Dan a chance to maneuver. Dan was able to sit in the "cone" between the two converging lines of fire that put bullets in both wings but not in his cockpit. A second's hesitation, one way or another, would have made the difference between life and death.

In the meantime, his Wing Man was in a low- level flight and was calling for help on his radio. Suddenly out of nowhere came four F6Fs who quickly chased the enemy fighters away. If those pilots had not come to their rescue, they probably would've had a very bad day. Later, he was asked if he had ever been shot down in combat and his comment was "I never got shot down---- just shot up".

On the way back to the Hornet Dan dug some shrapnel out of his legs with his knife. He really wasn't wounded. He says it was like the cinders you get when you fall on a running track.
He had no radio and no hydraulics but some way, somehow, he crashed landed safely on the Hornet. They cannibalized his plane for parts they needed and rolled the rest over the side into the ocean. It wasn't just junk, but it would have taken too long to repair it.

Over the next few months Dan flew missions over Okinawa and Kyushu. Their flight operations consisted mainly of picket duty north of Okinawa to intercept the kamikaze's flying down from Kyushu. They would be positioned above one of the "picket" destroyers and would be under the control of that destroyer. Those destroyers on that picket line took a terrible beating from the kamikazes. Many were sunk or very badly damaged. (Read story of Navy veteran Milt Mapou)

They also flew many fighter- sweeps and strikes over Kyushu, the large southern island of the Japanese mainland. Some of the American fighters engaged enemy fighters, but not Dan.
From Guam they continued their trip to Tacloban on Leyte in the Philippines, where they were to be relieved and returned to the States.

Dan was credited with 13 downed Japanese aircrafts (6M2 Zero) while serving in the Navy Air Corps.

In late 1945, Daniel A. Carmichael, Jr. was released from active duty

POST WAR ACTIVITIES

Dan remained active in the Naval Reserve serving two tours as the Commanding Officer of a jet fighter squadron and also flying as a Navy acceptance test pilot. In the mid-50s he retired as a Captain.

In 1947, Dan married the beautiful Patricia Tichenor and they brought into the world their children Tracy, Dan and Sally. Today, they have four wonderful grandchildren. Dan pursued architecture and was the leader of one of the most prestigious architectural firms in the Midwest. He designed many hospitals including the master plan for The OSU Medical Center. In 1966, he designed the Golf Club, one of the finest clubhouses in the country to this day.

His competitive and athletic spirit never waned. He won the Ohio State Amateur Golf Championship as well as becoming a two- time Ohio State Senior Golf Champion. He qualified 14 times for the National Amateur Golf Tournament. He was an avid handball player and racecar driver. He is a two-time Columbus Senior handball champion and in 1995, at the age of 77, he won the auto racing SCCA formula Atlantic National Championship.

WHAT OTHERS HAVE TO SAY ABOUT DAN

Tom Lynch:

Dan had a unique sense of humor. It wasn't "Ha, Ha" in your face sense of humor but he enjoyed a good laugh.

Dan had many wonderful qualities: humility, kind, loving, thoughtful, caring, forgiving, gentle: not boastful or self – seeking, generous, competitive, strong, goal oriented; good family man and quietly spiritual.

Greg Lashutka:

The treasured moments for me were conversations over a meal with Dan. I valued each occasion and left feeling good about life.

We both loved our country and wanted the best for the generations to follow us. Dan occasionally shared poignant reflections on his life including his military service.

Larry Snyder:

I never knew him to criticize or demeanor another person.

He once told me that on July 4th, because his old dog was terrified of the fireworks, he put him in his car, closed the windows, turned on the air conditioning and drove around for a couple of hours until the noise subsided. He was that kind of guy and that's how I will remember him.

Jack Stephan:

My first recollection of Dan dates back to 1946 when I was playing basketball at the Columbus Academy. During Christmas break we had an alumni/varsity game and Dan was playing for the alumni, most of whom who had just returned from the service in

World War II. All I remember about the game was that Dan dribbled the ball down the court six times, shot the ball from mid – court each time and made all six shots. No wonder the Japanese didn't have a chance.

Guy Fracasso:

One day I was practicing my handball skills at the Athletic Club when in walked Danny Carmichael. He asked me if I wanted to play a game. I told him I was not very good but I could use the practice. He beat me 21 to ZERO. The game lasted 8 minutes. He walked off the court and simply said "keep practicing". Apparently, he doesn't take prisoners!!! I loved him.

AWARDS AND RECOGNITION

- Silver Star Medal with one Gold Star (2)
- Distinguished flying Cross with three Gold Star (5)
- Air Medal with one Silver Star (13)
- Presidential Unit Citation awarded USS Hornet
- American Campaign Medal
- WWII Victory Medal
- Asiatic-Pacific Company Medal

- Philippine liberation Ribbon
- Gold Star
- American Fighter ACES Association
- Ohio Military Hall of Fame
- Ohio Golf Hall of Fame
- City of Columbus Hall of Fame
- Columbus Academy Athletic Hall of Fame

In 2003, Dan was awarded the LONE SAILOR AWARD which is given to Sea Service Veterans have excelled with distinction in their respective civilian careers while exemplifying the Navy core values of honor, courage and commitment.

On July 31, 2014 Dan passed away- His legacy and good deeds will live forever!

DANIEL CARMICHAEL-THANK YOU FOR YOUR SERVICE

Lieutenant Leila Allen Morrison

Leila Morrison was born on July 9, 1922 in Blue Ridge, Georgia. She had two sisters and four brothers of which she was the next to youngest. She graduated from Blue Ridge High School and followed her dream graduating from Baroness Erlander Nursing School in Chattanooga, Tennessee in 1943 at the age of 22. Soon after graduation she passed her State Boards of Nursing. In 1943, everyone was caught up in the war effort and all of her male friends were either drafted or had enlisted in the Armed Forces. Everyone wanted to serve our nation in some way. One day, she was talking with a US Army recruiter and he said "we need nurses in the worst way. If you don't volunteer, we are going to have to draft you and that would be an insult to the nursing profession". Leila remembers the conversation, "I fell for it at the time. I don't think I would now".

Leila volunteered for the US Army Air Corps at age 22. She completed training at Lowery Field in Denver before being sent to Santa Ana Army base for additional training. Later, she was transferred to the regular Army and then to the 10th field hospital at Camp Bowie in Brownwood, Texas. When she arrived in Texas, she discovered that she was one of 16 nurses who were to be deployed overseas. While training at Camp Bowie she learned map reading, logistics, bivouac and overall survival tactics that were essential for the combat zone she would be going to.

Leila and her brother

In early 1944 Leila and her fellow nurses boarded the Queen Elizabeth for England. Upon arriving they continued training in anticipation of the invasion of

Normandy and their future trek through Europe. In May, on small ships, they headed across the English Channel to Normandy. Upon arriving on June 11,1944, five days after the initial invasion, they were unable to land on shore because of all the disabled ships and landmines littering the shorelines and beaches. Leila with forty doctors and thirty-nine of her fellow nurses boarded landing craft boats which guided them to the shores of Normandy. On shore there were 2 ½ ton trucks which took the doctors and the nurses from place to place where they would set up evacuation hospitals (emergency room facilities).

They didn't know exactly where they were because they traveled at night and aided the sick and wounded during the day. She said they were always somewhere but nowhere. The devastation caused by war was horrendous.

They followed the troops wherever they were needed. In the winter months of 1944- 1945 she aided the sick and wounded at the Battle of the Bulge which was the largest battle fought by the Americans in World War II. 600,000 American troops were

 involved in the battle. The Americans lost 81,000 men while the Germans lost 100,000. Leila said the primary duty of a nurse was to aid soldiers who were in shock and prepare them for surgery.

Nothing could prepare Leila for what came next. HORROR!!!!!!!!!!

Buchenwald Concentration Camp April 1945

In 1937, Buchenwald was a Nazi concentration camp established on Ettersberg hill near Weimar, Germany. It was one of the first and largest of the concentration camps within Germany's borders. Buchenwald housed an estimated 266,000 prisoners. Many actual or suspected communists were among the first internees. Prisoners from all over Europe and the Soviet Union – Jews, Poles, and other Slavs, the mentally ill and physically disabled, political prisoners, Romani people, Freemasons, criminals, homosexuals, and prisoners of war worked primarily as forced labor in local armaments factories. It was essentially a death camp. Leila later learned how the Nazis disposed of those bodies when she toured the crematorium, inside a large building with two, triple – muffle ovens in the center. In the basement, there were more than 1,000 urns with the remains of the prisoners cremated there. All she could think was "this is a factory of murder".

The primary cause of death was illness due to harsh camp conditions, such as starvation and its consequent illnesses. Malnourishment and suffering from various diseases was prevalent. Many were literally "worked to death" under the extermination through labor mandate. The inmates had the choice between slave labor or inevitable execution. Many inmates died as a result of human experimentation or fell victim to arbitrary acts perpetrated by the SS guards. Other prisoners were simply murdered, primarily by shooting and hanging. The camp was also a site of large – scale trials for vaccines against epidemic typhus. One Nazi doctor's defense was that, although a doctor, he was a "legally appointed executioner". The total number of deaths at Buchenwald is estimated at 56,545.

A detachment of troops of the US 9th Armored Infantry Battalion, from the 6th Armored Division, part of the US third Army, and under the command of Capt. Frederick Keefer, arrived at Buchenwald on April 11, 1945 at 3:15 PM. The soldiers were given a hero's welcome, with some survivors finding the strength to toss some of the liberators into the air in celebration. Several journalists arrived on the same day, including Edward R. Murrow, who issued a radio report entitled "they died 900 a day in `the Best` *Nazi* death camp. Gen. George S. Patton toured the camp on April 15, and ordered the mayor of Weimar to bring 1,000 citizens to Buchenwald; these were to be prominent men of military age from the middle and upper classes. The Germans had to walk 16 miles round-trip under armored American guards and were shown the crematorium and other evidences of Nazi atrocities. The Americans wanted to ensure that the German people would take responsibility for Nazi crimes, instead of dismissing them as atrocity propaganda.

The doctors and Leila with the other nurses set up camp (tents) near the entrance of Buchenwald. The soldiers, who always worried about the nurses being so close to the front, were trying to shield them from the "deplorable" conditions of the camp. However, on the second day of liberation, the nurses were allowed to enter the camp. The prisoners were so emaciated Leila couldn't believe what she was witnessing. She said we use the expression – "skin and bones" – but these poor people, they weren't even that. The atrocities were unbelievable and unthinkable. She was heartbroken, but not unbroken.

I asked Leila how she handled the stress and trauma of working and aiding these concentration camp victims. This had to be an exhausting effort. Her response was quite revealing "I was young with lots of energy".

After the liberation and repatriation at Buchenwald the nurses achieved the distinction of being "seasoned troops" which meant they would be one of the first contingent of soldiers to come home. Welcomed news!!!!!!

Back to the United States

Leila boarded a troop ship in France and headed back to the New York Harbor. The war in Europe had ended on May 8, 1945. She was granted a 30 days furlough followed by 30 days of further training in preparation for the invasion of Japan. However, on August 6th and 9th (1945) America dropped atomic bombs on Hiroshima and Nagasaki and Japan surrendered. Leila believes that had we invaded Japan it would have cost 1 ½ million American casualties. She said that she always felt and prayed that GOD was on our side and that we would win the war. Her prayers came true.

Now that the war was over, it was time to get back to civilian life. Leila was discharged on August 15, 1945. Leila and her future husband Walter first met at the field hospital at Camp Bowie in Brownwood, Texas before departing for Europe. The day she arrived at Camp Bowie, Leila and the other 15 nurses who had been transferred from the Air Corps learned the officers of the 13th Armored Division were hosting a dance at the Brownwood Country Club; and they were short females. Leila and the girls agreed to be their dates. When the girls exited their barracks, two officers fought over Leila. She went with the second, a man by the name of Walter Morrison, Jr., because she liked his looks. By the end of their first date, Walter professed his love and asked Leila to marry him. "I told him he was acting foolish". I wasn't going to marry anyone while a war was going on." By chance Leila and Walter ran into each other while both were serving in Europe. Walter was with Patton's 3rd US Army.

After being discharged from the service they reunited and celebrated the first V-J day. That same day Walter again proposed "you promised you would marry me when the war was over". This time she said yes.

After their marriage they moved to Dallas, Texas and subsequently resided in Denison, Iowa where they raised their two daughters and son. They have six grandchildren and one great granddaughter. Walter owned and operated a radio station in Denison and Leila was a home maker but never gave up nursing. Leila says she liked staying home as a full-time mother because no one would spoil her kids as well as she could. Sadly, after 65 years of marriage Walter passed away in 2011.

Leila is a caregiver. She likes to serve others and to save lives. As a nurse, in a war zone, she dealt with trauma on a daily basis. In many cases she became a surrogate mother, sister, grandmother to the wounded soldiers she aided. Once she prepared the wounded for surgery, she never saw them again. She says to this day she wonders who made it and who didn't.

Today, Leila lives in an independent senior living community north of Denver, Colorado enjoying a peaceful but fulfilling life. She is very self- sufficient. Recently, at age 96, she flew alone to Phoenix, Arizona to visit her grand-niece.

As a result of a committed career as an Army nurse Leila was awarded:

- The Good Conduct Medal
- Medal of Occupation
- European Theater of Operation/2 Battle Stars

The French Legion of Honor

On February 4, 2019 Leila Allen Morrison was awarded the highest French order of merit for military and civil merits, established in 1802 by Napoleon Bonaparte and retained by all later French governments and regimes. She is decorated as Knights of the Legion of Honor. This award recognizes the commitment and dedication that Leila performed on the battlefields of France. Such an honor is awarded to only those individuals who showed courage and valor in the face of danger. Other American recipients include Gen. Dwight D. Eisenhower and Douglas

Leila wearing her Legion of Honor Award

MacArthur, and even, the United States military Academy at West Point.

Leila is a role model for all the world to admire!

LEILA MORRISON – THANK YOU FOR YOUR SERVICE

Milton Mapou

(This story was originally written by Ron Albers, and appeared in his article "Milton Maypou" and is provided by Motts Military Museum)

Milton was born on October 15, 1921 and raised in Rockaway Beach, N.Y. in the southern part of Queens. His father was a chauffeur for an executive on Park Avenue, and his mother worked part-time at a local bakery. Although Milt grew up during the great depression, it didn't seem to affect him and his siblings. "We always had food on the table and a roof over our heads." He was just trying to survive like most of the other kids in his neighborhood. When he attended public school, he sometimes had to insert cardboard in the soles of his worn- out shoes. On various occasions his school provided newer shoes that had been donated for the students.

Milt recalls nothing unusual or noteworthy about his childhood or years at Rockaway Beach Public Schools, where he also graduated from high school. It was war time and jobs were not available, so a logical option was to enlist in the military. He volunteered and was inducted into the US Navy on February 6, 1940 at the Federal Building in downtown New York City. From that swearing – in ceremony, he and others were marched down to the river for a twenty-four- hour boat ride to Providence, Rhode Island. At that point they were bussed to Newport, Rhode Island for a few months of basic training. Having been raised near the Atlantic Ocean, he knew how to swim, and he truly pitied the recruits who couldn't. Many were terrified as they were thrown in the water, but it was obviously a mandatory part of Navy basic training.

Following basic training, Milt was allowed two weeks of leave. He spent the time at home before being shipped to Boston. As a Boatswain's Mate, his duties included cleaning, painting, and maintaining the vessel's hull, superstructure and deck equipment as well as executing a formal preventive maintenance program. He spent a week working aboard the USS Constitution while awaiting orders for his next assignment which was the USS Dixie, a brand-new destroyer tender that could *repair nearly any vessel while in the open sea. The Dixie and her crew* had a leisurely cruise down through the Panama Canal and back up to San Diego. This trip took a few weeks as they often stopped at various ports to show off the beautiful new ship. Milt remained in San Diego for a week while the Dixie was refueled and restocked before heading to Hawaii.

Upon arrival at Pearl Harbor, Milt transferred from the Dixie and was given a job on an Admiral's- Staff. In November 1941, Milt was again assigned as part of the work deck force aboard the USS Detroit, a light cruiser which was docked at Ford Island in the middle of Pearl Harbor. On the **"day of infamy, December 7,1941"** most of the officers assigned to the Detroit were on weekend passes in Honolulu.

Just prior to 8 AM on Sunday morning, December 7, 1941, Milt and a pal had gotten their breakfast trays filled and were ready to sit down and eat when the Japanese attack occurred. They immediately rushed topside on the ship's port side and looked to see what was happening. Suddenly, Milt saw a plane turning to dive at them and he recognized the solid red ball painted on the fuselage. The Japanese were attacking them! Milt bellowed **"Where are our Officers when we need them?"** In an instant the pilot released his torpedo, which skimmed across the bow but missed and struck the shore. The plane passed so low over the Detroit that Milt could see the pilot's scary face.

Milt quickly moved to a large gun mount station, but it was pretty much worthless against a plane attack. From his vantage point Milt could watch the horrible destruction unfolding before him. He witnessed the nearby war ships Raleigh and Utah being sunk and the Nevada being run ashore after she was struck. The whole melee took less than two hours, but his ship, the Detroit, remained undamaged. After a brief wait to get the officers back aboard, the Detroit went to sea on patrol to search for enemy ships or subs but none were found. After two days they returned to Pearl to refuel and restock. The memories of that vicious attack by the Japanese has been seared in Milt's mind. Even after 77 years his emotions run cold when he relives that dastardly event.

Soon Milt and the USS Detroit were at sea again, this time escorting the Matsonia lines luxury liner filled with wounded servicemen and family members back to San Francisco. Then it was back to Pearl Harbor, where a US submarine had arrived from the Philippines filled with "gold and treasures" which needed to be kept away from the enemy. Once they were loaded aboard the Detroit, she again headed for San Francisco with her valuable cargo.

Upon arrival in San Francisco, Milt and a half dozen other seamen were assigned to the Treasure Island Naval Base. They were soon joined by others and bussed to a San Francisco train station. Before departing California, their rail car was hooked to an army troop train and they then headed for Chicago. In Chicago, Milt and the other seamen boarded another train that took them to the Navy Yard at Charleston, South Carolina. Upon arrival, this experienced crew was assigned to a brand-new Fletcher – class destroyer, the USS Pringle DD – 477. This was a uniquely – designed ship that had, on the stern, a catapult with a single seaplane aboard.

On New- Year's day of 1943, the USS Pringle departed on its first mission, a trip into the Atlantic to search for German U– boats and also to escort a contingent fleet from the European theater back to Halifax, Nova Scotia. They refueled and resupplied before returning to Charleston. While harbored in the Naval shipyard, the Pringle's captain let it be known that he wasn't pleased with the seaplane apparatus aboard his ship, and was able to convince the Navy to remove the plane and replace it with another large gun.

In January, 1943 the Pringle headed for the Panama Canal, where it joined a British aircraft carrier, the HMS Victorious (code- named USS Robin by the U.S. Navy – after the infamous Brit., Robin Hood), which Pringle then safely escorted across the Pacific to Pearl Harbor. At Pearl Harbor the Pringle was restocked and refueled. On February 6, 1943, they got underway for the battles in the Pacific. Arriving off Guadalcanal a few days later, the Pringle assumed patrol duties off the Solomon Islands, where they remained until September. The Pringle had a number of sea victories and also shot down several Japanese planes. The ship's success was vital to blocking the Japanese resupply lines.

Nine months later on November 11th, while escorting task group 31.7 into Empress Augusta Bay, Bougainville, the Pringle shot down one Japanese plane and damaged another. With the exception of a run to Sydney in late January 1944, they continued to operate in the Solomon's laying land mines at night for the next few months. They swept the southwest coast of Bougainville during daylight in early March of 1944 bombarding enemy installations and beached barges.

The Marianas operation produced another long period of bombardment, screening, and anti—submarine missions for the Pringle. During the assaults on Saipan and Tinian, they conducted fire support operations. Soon afterwards they returned to San Francisco, California, for refit and to rest their crew.

After overhaul at Mare Island Naval Shipyard, the Pringle sailed for Pearl Harbor on October 19, 1944. She departed Pearl Harbor on November 10th for the Philippines to take part in the upcoming invasion.

The Pringle came under her most intense air attacks while escorting a supply echelon to Mindoro. Several ships in the convoy were sunk. The Pringle shot down two planes. On November 30th, a Kamikaze crashed into Pringles aft deckhouse, killing 11 men and injuring 20, totally destroying one 40 mm mount and damaging two 5 -inch mounts.

Milton was manning one of the 5"/38 guns at the time. A piece of shrapnel pierced the mount and struck him in the back of the head. Another man in the same mount was killed instantly. For a day or two, Milt thought his injury was severe enough to allow him to be reassigned to duty on land. However, he was treated aboard ship before being assigned his duties once again. Meanwhile, the Pringle needed extensive repairs to make her battle worthy once again.

Back in service in February 1945, the Pringle screened transports to Iwo Jima for the invasion, then provided fire support for the Marines ashore. Incidentally, Milt **was able to see the raising of the American flag on Mt. Suribachi.** Returning to Ulithi on March 4th, they prepared for the assault of Okinawa.

Operating with Destroyer Division 90, they screened transport areas, covered minesweepers and provided support fire. On April 15th, the Pringle was assigned to "radar picket duty" (monitoring the skies and ocean for Japanese, not far from the coast of Okinawa). The very next day they shot down two kamikazes before a third crashed into her bridge, and plowed through the superstructure deck, just aft of number one stack. A single 1000-pound bomb penetrated the main and superstructure decks and exploded with a violent eruption, buckling the keel and splitting the vessel in two at the forward fire room. Six minutes later, 258 sailors watched the USS Pringle slide beneath the surface. Another 80 men had perished.

Milton was fortunate to be among the survivors. At
the time of the hit, he was manning a 40 mm gun
mount, and everything around him was demolished.
Death and destruction surrounded him. He was
wounded and knocked out. When he regained
consciousness, he noticed the bone of his right femur
sticking out, and his foot pointing backwards. A
fellow seaman inflated Milt's life jacket and yelled
"I'm sorry! That's all I can do!" before jumping
overboard. Milt couldn't move. Fortunately, the
bridge was rapidly filling with water which made it
possible for him to roll into the water. Somehow,
unbeknownst to Milt, he was able to get far enough
away from the Pringle so that he wasn't sucked under
when she sank.

A life raft appeared and Milt grabbed it. Someone gave him a shot of morphine and held onto him. The enemy planes were still overhead, but American planes quickly arrived to shoot down or chase away the enemy warbirds. He was in the water for about 2 ½ hours before the life raft was rescued by the USS Hobson. Medics aboard did what they could to save his life and leg while the destroyer headed for Okinawa. Upon arrival, Milt was transported to the hospital ship USS Hope and underwent a lengthy operation. From there he was taken to an Army hospital in Saipan, where they encased him in a body cast from his upper chest to the bottom of his feet. He remained at this facility for several weeks before they could air lift him aboard a C – 47 back to Pearl Harbor to a Quonset Hut Naval Hospital where he remained for several months. **Wounded but alive!!! His life was forever changed as a result of a shattered leg!**

While still in a full body cast eventually Milt was shipped back to the Oakland Navy Hospital in California. Prior to his arrival, his parents had relocated from Rockaway Beach, New York to California to be closer to his brother and sister who were in the military and stationed on the west coast. His brother was in the Air Corps and his sister was an Army Nurse.

The Japanese surrendered; and World War II ended on August 14, 1945. Milt remained in the hospital and was released and discharged on August 28, 1946.

"Join the Navy and See the World"

In 1940, at age 19, I can assure you that Milt could not have imagined what he was going to see and experience.

Chronological Travel

- Newport, Rhode Island for basic training
- Cruised down through the Panama Canal and back up to San Diego.
- Across the Pacific Ocean to Pearl Harbor
- **Experienced first- hand – "the day of infamy-December 7,1941"**
- Escorted wounded servicemen back to San Francisco
- Again, back to Pearl Harbor
- Again, headed for San Francisco
- Train trip from San Francisco to Chicago, Illinois
- Train trip from Chicago, Illinois to the Navy Yard at Charleston, South Carolina
- Mission- to the Atlantic to search for U-boats and also to escort a contingent fleet from the European theater back to Halifax, Nova Scotia
- Return trip to Charleston, South Carolina
- Return trip from Charleston back to Pearl Harbor

- Underwent battles in Guadalcanal, Bougainville and the Solomon Islands
- An excursion to Sydney Australia
- Assaults at Saipan and Tinian.
- Returned to San Francisco
- Returned to Pearl Harbor
- Departed for the Philippines
- Screened transports to Iwo Jima
- Prepared for the assault of Okinawa.
- His ship destroyed at sea
- Wounded – hospital ship for lengthy surgical operation in Saipan.
- Airlifted back to Pearl Harbor
- Shipped back to Oakland Navy Hospital, California

VARIOUS SHIPS

- USS Constitution-Heavy Frigate
- USS Dixie-Destroyer Tender
- USS Detroit- Light Cruiser (Pearl Harbor, December 7, 1941)
- USS Pringle- Fletcher Class Destroyer (blown apart by kamikazes)
- USS Hopson- Gleaves Class Destroyer
- USS Hope-Hospital Ship

MEDALS

- Purple Heart w/Gold Star
- Asiatic/Pacific Campaign Medal w/9 Stars
- Defense Service Medal w/Star

BACK TO CIVILIAN LIFE

In 1940, when Milton enlisted in the Navy, he envisioned a career in the service. However, the fact that he was severely wounded ended that dream. As Milt expressed to me "when you're shot up – you are unfit for sea duty – you are out".

After being discharged from the Navy Milt traveled from California, to New York City, to Florida and back to California seeking employment. Potential employers shied away from him because of his damaged leg. Without work his only source of income was the disability check that he received from the government. From time to time he was able to gain employment in the shipping departments of clothing and shoe manufacturers. In 1977 he met and married his wife Helen.

In the late 1980s he and Helen finally decided to retire, leave California and move back to Helen's hometown of Columbus Ohio. In 2006, after 29 years of marriage Helen passed away. Today, Milt has two step sons and four grandchildren.

Milt survived the attack on Pearl Harbor and the subsequent sinking of his ship and today remains a Navy veteran proud of his service to the United States of America. On December 7, 2018, Milt at age 97, was one of about 20 survivors who gathered at Pearl Harbor to pay tribute to the thousands of men lost in the Japanese attack 77 years ago. Duty called once again.

When I asked Milt about his time serving in the Navy his response was understated as usual "I did my job as best as possible, had a great experience and have no regrets". Milt spent every Wednesday and Saturday volunteering at the Motts Military Museum in Groveport, Ohio.

MILTON MAPOU- THANK YOU FOR YOUR SERVICE

In Memoriam

Sadly, on January 17, 2019 Milton passed away peacefully at age 97. His service as a World War II Navy Veteran helped keep the United States a symbol for freedom. A true war hero.

MILTON MAPOU- MAY YOU REST IN PEACE

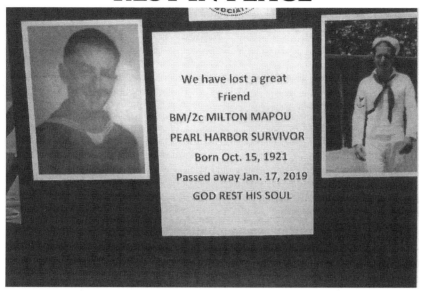

We have lost a great
Friend
BM/2c MILTON MAPOU
PEARL HARBOR SURVIVOR
Born Oct. 15, 1921
Passed away Jan. 17, 2019
GOD REST HIS SOUL

PFC Edwin T. Leibbrand

Eddie Leibbrand was born in Columbus, Ohio on January 27, 1924 and was a youngster during the great depression. Raised on Jenkins Avenue, his father dug ditches for the WPA. Eddie had three sisters but lost an older brother who died at the age of six from diphtheria. Young Eddie attended schools in Columbus: Southwood Elementary, Barrett Junior High School and South High School. During his high school years Eddie developed mastoiditis, a serious disease in those days caused by an untreated inner ear infection. As a result, he missed a year of high school.

In 1943, on the 30th of January Eddie was drafted out of high school (which he never completed.) At 98

North High street in downtown Columbus he was given a physical examination. Eddie was disqualified because of a bad right eye. He had developed a problem with his eye as a result of a childhood bout with whooping cough. When he saw the final doctor at the end of the physical examination process, the doctor noted that he'd been rejected due to the eye problem. Instead of releasing Eddie, the doctor told him to get back in line and repeat the process. Of course, Eddie complied; and this time he passed the physical. There was a great demand for soldiers.

Eddie was granted a month to get his affairs in order and then taken by train to camp Atterbury, Indiana, where he was inducted on March 1st and received a week of indoctrination. Next, he was sent to Camp Walters, Texas for basic training. During his six weeks there he was instructed in the specialty of machine gunner, specifically the Browning.30 caliber water – cooled machine-gun. The weapon could fire 450 to 600 rounds per minute, and a typical magazine belt held 250 rounds. At the end of his training, his unit was deployed to Alaska; but due to a problem with his eyeglasses, Eddie remained behind and was reassigned to Pennsylvania's 110th Regiment of the 28th Infantry Division at Camp Kilmer, New Jersey, in preparation for their deployment to Europe.

Departing from pier 98 in New York City on April 17, 1944, the 110th was aboard the Queen Elizabeth, a ship that could hold nearly 10,000 troops. Also, on board were Bing Crosby and Bob Hope and their entourage. They put on a number of shows for the troops during their eight- day voyage across the Atlantic.

Upon their arrival in England, Private Leibbrand and the other members were housed in Quonset buildings for several weeks where they were issued equipment and practiced for the combat situations they would face when they reached mainland Europe. Eddie received specific training to keep him current on maintaining and firing his water cooled.30 caliber Browning machine gun. The troops of the 110th where ferried across the English Channel on Higgins Boats. Upon arriving at Le Havre that September, the 110th was again quartered in Quonset huts nearby for the next two weeks, where they were issued additional equipment, received final training, and continued to prepare for battle.

The Battle of the Bulge
POW Nazi Stalag 98

Eddie and his fellow troops then marched across France doing "cleanup duties" to root any remaining Germans from their hiding places. They proudly participated in the liberation of Paris before continuing their fight across France and into

Belgium, Luxembourg, and Germany. One day they were transported by train back to a town in Belgium and posted in a "holding position." The soldiers ate and slept in the homes of the town they had surrounded and fortified, and they rotated shifts to guard the town. Early in December, 1944 a massive number of German tanks and troops had them completely surrounded and ferociously attacked. **It was the first Nazi offenses of the Battle of the Bulge. More than 2,700 men of the 110th were lost in three days and nights of fierce combat, while the 110th caused an equal number of casualties among the Germans.**

While trying to regroup, the Americans asked a young German lad where the best place to rendezvous would be. Unbeknownst to them, this boy was apparently a Nazi sympathizer. His directions took them to a nearby field with a number of American tanks. Unfortunately for Eddie and his fellow soldiers, those tanks were disabled; and the field was enmeshed with hiding Nazi troops, who quickly surrounded the Americans and began mowing them down. Our guys who were still standing had no choice but to surrender. And they did. Eddie was captured on December 18, 1944. On the day Eddie and his fellow troops were captured the Germans lined them up in front of a German tank with a 50- caliber machine gun staring them in the face. Eddie turned to the soldier next to him and said "it was nice knowing you – we will be dead soon". However, fate intervened as a high-ranking German officer ordered his men not to execute them but to march them to a POW prison camp –Stalag 9B where he remained for the next four months in sub- freezing weather.

For a number of days, the captured Americans were marched by day, sleeping in schools and churches at night. Along the way, a "Hitler youth" young girl sniper shot him in his leg. As a side note, Eddie did not receive the Purple Heart because he was not wounded in battle. They were giving nothing to eat or drink, and the cold weather was unbearable. The soldiers huddled together while sleeping in masses to share and preserve body heat. At one time Eddie recalls wondering why the 300 or so prisoners were continually marched in a huge circle through this one particular village. Later it was learned from a German newspaper that the Nazis had declared that they had captured more than 450,000 Allied troops; and by continuingly marching the prisoners past the same area, the Nazis, hoped to convince the Belgians that indeed they had captured a substantial number and were winning the war.

For the final four days of this trek he and his fellow prisoners were crammed into "40&8" railroad cars. These French railroad cars were so nicknamed because they were designed with the intent of carrying 40 men and 8 horses. Of course, the Germans crammed as many as 100 prisoners of war (POWs) into each of these cars. Still no food or water. The cars remained locked, and the bathroom was a guy's helmet, which was emptied through holes in the floor. The trains travel at night to avoid being strafed by American planes. During the day, they simply parked in the freezing cold. The Americans were becoming weaker, ill, and dying. At one stop, one of the soldiers managed to open the door to allow some fresh air into the car. A German guard promptly shot the POW in the head with his Luger and closed the door again.

Eddie will tell you that he believes in the power of prayer. Even though it was too crowded to kneel, standing together, they all prayed for some food. Within two or three hours, the prisoners were given some rations to sustain them.

Finally, they arrived at their destination – Stalag 9B at Bad Orb, Hessen, Germany – just north east of Frankfurt. History has recorded it as being the worst of all the Nazi POW camps. The camp was a virtual concentration camp that held low ranking captives from the US., England, Russia, Serbia, and France.

There were only three officers in the camp, two chaplains and a dentist. Everyone else was a private or PFC. When the men were liberated on April 2, 1945, there were 6000 prisoners released including 3,364 Americans. The camp was extremely primitive. The men slept on straw mats infested with lice. There were not any medical facilities or sanitary services.

No heat, and very little grass or potato soup. Showers were rare, and following one, the men had to dress once again in their same dirty clothing. Men died every day from dehydration, malnutrition, hypothermia, or a variety of illnesses. Eddie's weight in the four months he was in Stalag 9B went from 160 pounds to 98 pounds. Such a weight loss (if one lived at all) was the norm. The conditions in this particular camp have been compared to those in the Jewish concentration camps. Being on top of a mountain with its resultant winds, made the camp extremely cold that winter. The POWs were never issued any clothing, and most arrived with only a field jacket. They had very few caps, gloves or overcoats. The only food he was given during his four-month stay was three small potatoes a day. Five to eight of his fellow comrades died each day.

The International Red Cross continually sent packages to these prisoners of Stalag 9B, but only a few of them ever arrived. Packages were found hoarded in storage in Bad Orb following the POW's repatriation. A twelve – pound package was supposed to provide a man with all his needs for a week. Eddie only recalls one time when Serbs brought a quarter of these packages for each man.

Also, the Red Cross had never sent a letter telling his family that he was missing in action. They had no idea if he was dead or alive. By pure coincidence, PATHE NEWS had filmed Eddie and his fellow prisoners being marched to their POW camp. Eddie's cousin was attending the local movie theater in Columbus, Ohio where he spotted Eddie as one of the prisoners. He ran home and excitedly told the family that Eddie was alive. This was the only communication the family had concerning Eddie's interment.

On one occasion a German guard was killed. Everyone in his Stalag was awakened in the middle of the night by storm troopers poking them in the butt with bayonets and forcing them outside into the freezing cold air and knee – high snow. Some had no shoes and very little clothing. They were told they would remain there until they told who had done the killing. The guards quickly found blood on one prisoners clothing, and the remainder were allowed back inside.

The POWs were continually forced to march down to the village of Bad Orb to cut and split firewood for the residents. Not usually being one to volunteer, at one -point Eddie volunteered for a project just to do something different from the daily routine and horrific conditions of the camp. After spending the entire night out in the freezing cold digging graves for fellow POWs who had died, he never volunteered again.

Another vivid memory of Eddie's occurred just prior to the liberation of the POWs from Stalag 9B. While standing in the camp's yard, a P-47 came streaking directly at him at extremely low level. Eddie could see right down the barrel of the .30 caliber machine gun and could plainly see the pilots face. Eddie thought he was dead! Suddenly, the plane zoomed away, its wings rocking. It seems the French prisoners spelled out "POW" on the ground in the limestone where the pilot saw it at the last moment before strafing the camp. Lucky again not to be killed!!!

The tanks of Patton's Army suddenly appeared the day after Easter in 1945 and didn't bother to enter through the gates of Stalag B. They simply drove over and through the barricades and fences into the camp. The guards put up no resistance. The Nazi's were aware that the inevitable would soon happen, and they promptly surrendered. Nearly as quickly, PFC Eddie Leibbrand collapsed face first onto the ground. His body could take no more. He was ravaged by extreme malnutrition and jaundice. He was evacuated to a hospital in France where it took three months of rehabilitation to bring him back to life. He then was taken to Camp Lucky Strike and issued the clothing necessary for his voyage back to the United States.

Departing from Le Havre, Eddie's return home was aboard a destroyer. He recalls that they were followed by a German submarine all the way into

New York Harbor which then surrendered. The date was August 1, 1945.

Eddie was treated to a wonderful 60 – day leave with his family in Columbus before being shipped by train to Miami Beach, Florida for two more weeks of R&R. While there he received orders to report to Fort Bragg, North Carolina, where he was trained on a 60mm mortar in preparation for his deployment to the Pacific Theater. Obviously, Eddie protested on the grounds that he had suffered enough as a POW in the war. After two weeks at Fort Bragg, Eddie was granted his appeal based on the point system. He was taken by train to Camp Atterbury, Indiana. Eddie recalls the train stopping at Columbus' Union Station, just a few miles from his home and family. He wasn't allowed off even for a brief visit, and he was heartbroken.

Personnel at Camp Atterbury completed his final out processing and granted his honorable discharge on November 28, 1945.

Upon returning to Columbus, Eddie discovered that houses were not readily available for purchase. Luckily for him he was able to live in the government-built Quadruplexes in the "Green Lawn Projects" just south of downtown Columbus. Adjusting to civilian life was difficult at first. For a number of years if he was awakened at night by the sound of an airplane over head he would dive under his bed. Those war memories as a POW were slow to forget.

He met his first wife at a bingo game, and he and Billie were married in 1946. They had one son. Meanwhile, Eddie worked for 10 years as a machine repair man on the C&O railroad, working on boilers and engines. His father also worked for the same company for 65 years, dying at age 104. Eddie spent the next 28 years working as a machinist at Columbus Bolt Works near the old penitentiary (now part of the Arena District).

In August 1981, Billie passed away from complications of diabetes and cardiac arrest. Eddie remarried again in July 1983 to Jane, a widow with two daughters who Eddie has always treated as his own. She passed away in December 2007, but Eddie remains close to his daughters, Paula Brown and Martha England, and his three grandchildren – Jessica, Carrie, and Jason.

In April 2007, the Pickerington High School honored veteran Eddie with an honorary high school diploma as a token of compensation for leaving high school before graduation to serve our nation during World War II. Eddie sincerely appreciated that gesture and still treasures that framed diploma.

LIFE TODAY

In 2019 Eddie enjoys living alone in a small home, with his dog and his memories. He does his own cooking and housecleaning. He is a man at peace today. As a prisoner of war Eddie receives a disability pension from the United States government. He drives a small Honda and scooter around Pickerington, Ohio where he visits the barbershop and the bank.

Admittedly, Eddie has lost some of his memory. Perhaps that's a good thing. What he does remember, however he is willing to share. At age 95, Eddie is still willing and able to tell you his story about his service during World War II. You may want to visit him on Wednesday afternoons at the Motts Military Museum. He has some great stories to tell about fighting in the Ardennes's, liberating Paris and becoming a prisoner of war.

When I asked Eddie if he felt he was a war hero. His response was simple and direct "war heroes are those who died on the battlefield for our freedom". He doesn't want anyone to think he was a war hero. He was an unfortunate victim of circumstances at times, but he did what he had to do; and he is proud of his service to our country. He doesn't look back at what might have been.

EDDIE LEIBBRAND-THANK YOU FOR YOUR SERVICE

1st. Lt. Michael J. Pohorilla

In February, 1943, at age 18, Mike Pohorilla enlisted in the Army Air Corps and looked forward to serving our country against evil and tyranny. Within a short period of time his brothers Emil and Vincent enlisted in the Navy. Emil fought at Normandy and his youngest brother, Vincent, served on an icebreaker in Greenland. The brothers came from a family with a strong military tradition. During World War I his father was with the 4th Infantry Division and was gassed during the campaign in Northern France. His father died of lung disease in 1928, but his mother was able to financially survive with her sons during the depression of the 1930s and by 1944 displayed a banner with three blue stars during World War II.

Mike was born on January 13, 1924 growing up in Kingston, Pennsylvania. His mother was a homemaker and his father worked in the coal mines. Mike attended Girard College High School in Philadelphia, Pennsylvania graduating in 1940. In February, 1943, he enlisted as an Aviation Cadet in the Army Air Corps. The Aviation Cadet program was designed to train 100,000 pilots a year to support the upcoming European invasions and the island-hopping campaigns of the Pacific Theater. Early in 1943, he traveled to basic training in Miami Beach, Florida at the age of 18 and was thrust into military life. It was a dramatic change of lifestyle for Mike. Basic training sequenced into Pre—Flight School at Maxwell Field in Montgomery, Alabama. The aviation cadet program produced close order drill and parades the equal of any service. In late summer of 1943, Mike was assigned to Primary Flight School operated by a civilian contract flight training school at Souther Field in Americus, Georgia. A bronze plaque memorialized Charles Lindbergh's flight training at this location. Mike soloed after the requisite eight hours dual instruction in a Stearman PT-17 biplane but was unable to pass a critical 40 – hour check ride. Given the urgency of turning out 100,000 pilots annually, Mike was not given a second chance.

Washing out as a pilot the Army assigned Mike to Navigator Flight School at Selman Field in Monroe,

Louisiana, but first there was a six weeks detour to earn his aerial gunner's wings at Fort Myers, Florida. Navigator school started in late 1943 which provided him with intensive ground and flight training in all the navigational arts available at that period – Dead reckoning, celestial and radio navigation and meteorology. There weren't any radar aids available until combat in Europe in the autumn of 1944.

Graduation in April, 1944 brought navigator's wings, new uniforms and second Lieut. bars. Then he was sent to operational training. Mike's B – 17 G flying fortress bomber crew was assembled at Sioux City, Iowa. They had a crew of four officers and six staff Sergeants from diverse backgrounds. Most of them were very young (18 – 20) men. The oldest was a 22-

year-old Michigan graduate who manned the tail gunner position. From April to June 1944, the crew learned the intricacies of close formation flying, long-range (500 – 600 miles) missions, gunnery training and bombing simulations all over the upper Midwest landscape. Orders to ship to Europe came about three weeks after D – DAY. Because there weren't any shortages of aircraft in the European theater, the crew traveled from the Brooklyn Navy Yard to Liverpool, England in convoy aboard a prewar Italian luxury liner along with 10,000 other servicemen. The liner, SS Saturnia, had sailed into North Africa and surrendered by its captain to the Allies prior to Italy's military collapse. Consequently, the ship's masthead flew the flags of both the Stars and Stripes and the Italian tricolor.

8th Air Force, 385th Bomb Group

In early July, they arrived in England and were immediately assigned to the 8th Air Force and the 385th Bomb Group (Heavy) which was located in a small East Anglican village, Elmswell, about 40 miles East of Cambridge. The base was known as Great Ashfield.

England had been at war for five years when Mike and his crew arrived. Blackouts and blackout window shades were mandatory. Severe food rationing was the norm and was reflected even in their spartan menus. Foul British weather in fall and winter with low ceiling, rain, frost and raw temperatures complicated both personal comfort and more critically combat flight operations. The one pleasure they had was listening to Major Glenn Miller's Air Force band over the BBC every evening at 7:00 PM, just like home.

Mike and his fellow crew members were gradually indoctrinated into combat flying by serving individually as members of a seasoned crew. It was not until each crewmember had flown several missions in this manner before the group finally went into combat as a unit. The combat tour was now 35 missions, having been increased from 25, then 30, as crew losses were gradually lowered as a result of fighter protection (Air Force P-51s). Mike's first baptism by fire was bombing the Daimler Benz home factory at a Stuttgart suburb (Sindelfingen) which was a major producer of tanks and aircraft engines. The crew initially flew various B – 17 aircrafts but soon they were assigned the "Sky Goddess" whose crew had completed their 35 mission tours. This great aircraft, having been battle tested, sported the usual female form nose art.

Unlike the Royal Air Force (RAF) Bomber Command which flew only night raids and practiced widespread area bombardment, the 8th Air Force was committed to precision daytime bombing. More importantly, the formation was designed to allow the group to salvo their bomb loads to strike within a 1,000- foot circle about the target. These tactics were attributed to Gen. Curtis LeMay, who at the time was deputy to Gen. Jimmy Doolittle, Commanding General of the 8th Air Force.

The fall – winter period of 1944 was the most intense combat period for the 8th Air Force. The strategic mission of the 8th Air Force was to destroy the German industrial complex which would starve the Reich's war machine. Mike and the "Sky Goddess" crew, from late August 1944 until February 1945, were preoccupied with destroying ordinance depots, tank and aircraft engine factories, Tiger Tank manufacturing facilities, steel plants, aircraft factories, major railroad marshaling yards and synthetic oil plants including its oil refineries. This latter period was particularly critical to the Reich because Germany did not have any indigenous oil assets. However, it did have coal, lots of it, and via a pressurized coal hydrogenation process it was able to produce streams of hydrocarbon, the lifeblood of the German war machine. Therefore, the 385th Bomb Group repeatedly visited installations at Ludwigshaven, Hamburg and Merseberg.

The constant strategic bombing tattoo carried Mike and the crew to centers of German industrial might including Stuttgart, Berlin, Cologne and Mannheim. They didn't miss many German locations. On Christmas eve, 1944, the 8th Air Force bombers tendered their support, bombing troop concentration, transportation hubs, Rhine bridges and tank depots.

There were 2,000 Air Force air craft in the air that day in support of the Battle of the Bulge.

The 8th Air Force daylight missions were carried out in a very hostile environment. The B- 17 and B- 24 aircrafts were not pressurized therefore the climate outside was the same as they endured inside the aircraft. Bombing altitude was generally 25,000 – 28,000 ft. with outside temperatures at -42 to-50 c. Combat operations had to be sustained with oxygen pressure at 25% of that experienced at sea level. Loss of life could occur in about two minutes should the airmen be deprived of oxygen. On one occasion the bombardier saw Mike sprawled on the floor unconscious, his oxygen mask off his face. He quickly replaced Mike's mask and turned his oxygen pressure valve up to the hundred percent setting. Mike quickly gained consciousness, stood for a few minutes, and advised his fellow crewmen that he was okay. Mike's oxygen mask had frozen due to the high humidity at -40 c. Crew discipline and the bombardier's quick action had saved Mike's life.

Collateral damage was minimal – Mike's bladder had emptied as completely as a diapered two-year-old and his head was banged up a bit as he fell. (No Purple Heart). He promptly turned the rheostat on his heated suit control to "maximum" to dry out and continued on with his routine tasks. Mike and his fellow crewmen survived the cold by the simple scheme of layering their clothing and an ingenious heated suit. Missions which lasted 6 to 9 hours, most of which were at high altitude, began at 4:30 AM–5:00 AM.

Dressing for the mission followed this typical sequence:
- Regular underwear
- Long johns
- Silk socks

- Wool socks
- Standard uniform
- Heated suit (4 piece)
- Nylon flight coveralls
- Insulated boots
- Mae West
- Flight helmet
- Parachute harness
- Flak jacket
- Escape packet
- .45 caliber Pistol

Breakfast before takeoff was always memorable because mission crews were served fresh eggs, any style.

The collective bond between the members of B-17 crews were close unlike any relationship experienced before or after World War II. Thus, the relationship between officers and enlisted men still existed, but within the crew it was somewhat softened. All 10 men each had specific tasks and survival depended upon total discipline during combat.

Critical targets in Germany were heavily defended by numerous 88 mm and 120 mm flak guns. The 88 mm weapon was generally regarded as the finest artillery piece of World War II. Over the targets the Germans placed a continuous barrage as to fill a hypothetical cube of airspace measuring 1000 feet top to bottom at bombing altitude and covering the length and breadth of the target area. Bombers simply had to plow through the forest of flak bursts while on their straight-line bombing runs.

When the 385th Bomb Group visited Merseberg in late September 1944, they encountered about 1,000 Flak guns. On November 25th Mike's plane, the Sky Goddess, dropped its 3 tons of 500- pound bombs from 27,500 feet but in the bombing raid flak disabled the number 3 starboard engine. There was a brief fire, but quickly snuffed out as the flight deck feathered the prop. The B – 17 can fly on two or three engines, but maintaining altitude becomes a problem. Specific fuel consumption goes through the roof. Sky Goddess limped along on three engines while maintaining a position close with the group formation. The fuel gauges dropped at an alarming rate. Mike finally announced that the plane's position over the Ardennes was within allied lines. He gave Wally, the pilot, a heading directly for Dover, England and the plane began a gradual descent, leaving the protection of the group formation.

Eventually, over southern Belgium, pilot Wally summoned Mike to the flight deck, advising him to assemble the crew midship. The fuel gauges were on "empty" and the alarm bell – abandon ship – would sound. Mike's task was to ensure that all the crew cleared the aircraft. He gave the order to snap on their parachutes and soon the alarm bell rang "Okay, you guys, jump". At the moment they were cruising at 1000 feet and everyone sensed that parachuting at that altitude was marginal. So, they all just stood silent. Mike hurried back to the flight deck. "Wally, these guys won't jump. We're too low. You'll have to set this baby down". The pilots selected a freshly plowed field and crashed landed about 40 miles southwest of Brussels. The plane gently settled, wheels up. No fuel left, no fire, no casualties. Mike and the other crew members hastily abandoned ship and Sky Goddess was left in Belgium. That was mission number 18 for the crew.

Mission number 19 was two weeks later, and psychologically it was the most difficult of the tour. The original crew survived 35 missions except for the waist gunner, who was lost while substituting with another crew. Missions later, number 35 occurred February 1, 1945. Mike said God was surely their copilot.

SACRIFICE

The US Army 8th Air Force consisted of 350,000 airmen which was the largest military unit in World War II. There were 26,000 killed in action and 20,000 taken as POW's. The 385th Bombardment Group (Heavy) flew 300 missions, losing 130 airplanes with 230 killed in action. The average combat life of a B – 17 was four months and 12 days. None of the original B – 17's survived World War II.

In March 1945, Mike came home on a hospital ship and was discharged from the service in October of the same year. On February 1, 1945 Michael Pohorilla was formally inducted into the "Lucky Bastard Club" testifying that he had achieved the remarkable record

of completing 35 air combat missions in Europe.

LIFE AFTER THE WAR

After becoming accustomed to post war life, Mike, with the aid of the G.I. Bill, enrolled at the University of Pennsylvania. He married his wife Ellen in 1947 and received his Master's Degree in Chemistry as a research Chemist in 1950. He gained employment with the Kendall Refining Company as Director of new product development and he was instrumental in developing and marketing the first 10 W 30 weight motor oil (multi-graded motor oils) in the United States. After 12 years with Kendall he joined Rohm and Haas Chemical Company which is now a part of Dow Chemical. He retired 25 years later as a successful Chemist and businessman.

Today, Mike, has two sons and many grand and great grandchildren. Unfortunately, Ellen passed away on January 1, 2000.

While visiting with Mike, I asked him a number of questions on a wide variety of subjects:

I asked him about his generation – "We stuck to it"

I asked him about the Greatest Generation during war – "We did our duty then came home"

I asked him about the G.I. Bill – "It created the greatest middle class in American history. Without it our servicemen couldn't have gone back to school".

I asked him if he considered himself a war hero – "No, I did my job and never thought about being a hero"

I asked him if the country had another crisis would he put on his uniform – "Yes or hell yes".

I asked what advice he had for the younger generation – "Love our country"

I asked Mike if he had any further advice – "Follow the fifth commandment – honor thy mother and father".

Mike was awarded a number of medals including 6 Air Medals, 3 Campaign Ribbons and a Victory Medal.

Mike Pohorilla, A True American War Hero!!!

MICHAEL POHORILLA-THANK YOU FOR YOUR SERVICE

FEEDBACK

Do you feel the World War II combat veterans you just read about are any different from you? If you were put into a perilous situation, like fighting in a war, how do you think you would perform? If interested in sharing your views please email me. Also, if you are a Veteran do you consider yourself a war hero?

dcohen1935@gmail.com

Photo courtesy of Motts Military Museum

Photo courtesy of Motts Military Museum

Motts Military Museum

The Motts Military Museum, located at 5075 South Hamilton Rd., Groveport, Ohio, houses a vast collection of stories and memorabilia which covers all of America's Military history from its founding right up to the present. The museum is a testament to those men and women who fought for the freedoms we enjoy today. You will be able to take all the time necessary to roam the 10,000 ft.² facility – it is simply fabulous!!!!

www.mottsmilitarymuseum.org
E- mail: **info@mottsmilitarymuseum.org**
Phone information: 614-836-1500

Warren Motts and daughter, Lorie

Shrapnel from the USS Arizona (Photo courtesy of Motts Military Museum)

Uniform from WW II Code Talkers (Photo courtesy of Motts Military Museum)

Ted Williams' baseball glove from his time as a U.S. Marine pilot (Photo courtesy of Motts Military Museum)

Uniform of Paul Tibbets - Pilot of the Enola Gay (Photo courtesy of Motts Military Museum)

Tuskegee Airmen display (Photo courtesy of Motts Military Museum)

Photo courtesy of Motts Military Museum

ABOUT THE AUTHOR AND PREVIOUS WRITINGS

After graduating from the Columbus Academy and Miami University, David began his career as an insurance agent and still continues this activity today. Back in the late 1970's, as a hobby, David learned the art of Chinese cooking and throughout the last number of years he and his wife, Rita, have entertained hundreds and hundreds of guests with their fabulous and delicious appetizers and main course dishes.

Today, his main focus is that of chronicling the lives of World War II combat veterans.

BOOKS:
- Get What You Want
- How I Got This Way
- Prospect or Perish
- Never Stop Prospecting
- Sorry, Downtown Columbus is Closed
- 1000 Years of Memories

PLAYS:
- A Couple of Kids Once More
- A Living History Saga

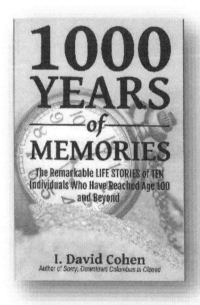

Made in the USA
Lexington, KY
06 November 2019